ENGLISH CHAIRS

One of a set of eight arm-chairs and four sofas made by Thomas Chippendale from
designs by Robert Adam for Sir Lawrence Dundas. About 1764. W.1 – 1937.

VICTORIA AND ALBERT MUSEUM

English Chairs

LONDON
HER MAJESTY'S STATIONERY OFFICE

LARGE PICTURE BOOK No. 10
© Crown copyright 1970
First published 1951
Third edition 1970
Second impression 1977

ISBN 0 11 290031 3

Foreword

THIS brief history of the English Chair was originally prepared by Mr Ralph Edwards, formerly Keeper of the Department of Woodwork, and was revised by Mr Desmond Fitz-Gerald, Assistant Keeper of the Department of Furniture and Woodwork in 1970.

A History of the English Chair

THOUGH movable chairs were certainly known in England before the Norman Conquest, they did not come into general use throughout the Middle Ages even in royal palaces and the castles of great nobles.[1] Settles, benches and stools were the ordinary seats, while chairs were regarded as symbols of authority reserved for the master of the house and distinguished guests: this symbolic significance long continued to attach to them, and is still commemorated by the term 'Chairman' for the person who takes his place at the head of a board. Down to early Georgian times a rigorous etiquette governed the use of chairs on ceremonial occasions at Court.

In medieval illuminated manuscripts throne-like structures resembling ecclesiastical stalls are sometimes shown standing against the walls in halls or chambers, with a 'dosser' or backing of tapestry or embroidered material behind the occupant and a 'banker' or cushion on the seat. A lighter variety often represented in illuminations (Fig. 1) was of X shape, a form which dates back to the early Middle Ages and was in use throughout Western Europe. References occur in inventories of the fifteenth century to 'Flaunders chairs' (part of a large traffic in foreign furniture) and to others made *Ad Modum Anglicanum*, but such terse descriptions do not suffice to determine their character. Turned or 'thrown' chairs are also found mentioned – a variety of great antiquity and wide geographical distribution which remained in favour until a much later date, the seats being triangular and the whole structure turned (Fig. 7). These were produced by the Turners, a trade guild whose existence can be traced from the beginning of the fourteenth century, though they did not obtain a charter of incorporation until 1604.[2]

The form of some of the earliest surviving domestic chairs shows them to have been evolved from the chest by the addition of a panelled back and sides. In the carving of Fig. 2, an important example of this small group of 'box-chairs', the linen-fold pattern that figures so frequently in late Gothic woodwork is combined with ornament in which Renaissance influence can be clearly discerned.

A chair first discovered in a Devonshire village (Fig. 3) is of the French type called *caquetoire* (*caqueter* to chatter) or *chaire de femme*, in allusion to the passion for gossip that is supposed to have popularized it. There are many chairs of this type in Continental collections (the Museum has two fine French examples)[3] exhibiting a considerable variety of design, but enquiry has failed to reveal the existence abroad of any close parallel. The blunt and summary handling of the foliated scrollwork and demi-terminal figures framing a woman's head in a lozenge, is characteristic of West Country carving. Chairs of similar pattern were certainly produced in England (Fig. 5); while the close alliance of the French and Scottish Crowns at this period caused the form to be adopted in Scotland. Among these early 'joyned' chairs should also be included the so-called 'Glastonbury' type (based on North Italian models), in which the back has a pronounced rake and the arms, shaped underneath, slope upwards to support the elbows (Fig. 6).

For the building and equipment of his new palaces Henry VIII employed a number of foreign artists and craftsmen: through their influence, England was brought into closer touch with the Renaissance and the more advanced civilization of the Continent. In the long lists of the king's possessions, drawn up after the accession of Edward VI (1547) many magnificent chairs are described, which, if not of foreign origin, were derived from French and Italian prototypes. Some were of walnut (a wood which now began to supplement the native oak) painted and gilded, while a number were of the traditional X shape with 'pomells', or finials of gilded wood or copper. The frames of such chairs were completely covered with silk or velvet trimmed with fringes glued down and secured by ornamental gilt nails; the seats consisting of loose cushions supported on webbing between the side rails. An 'X chair', of which the condition recalls the description 'sore worne' in a contemporary inventory, is still preserved in Winchester Cathedral, and is said to have been used by Mary Tudor at her marriage to Philip of Spain: in their portraits the Queen and great courtiers are shown seated in chairs of this kind.[4] But such luxuries were in no way representative of the general standard of furnishing, and contemporary inventories prove that even in large houses chairs were still greatly outnumbered by stools.

The familiar panel-back type of joined chair came into general use towards the end of the sixteenth century. Made of oak and more rarely of walnut, they were sometimes inlaid in a variety of coloured wood (box, holly, bog-oak and sycamore being the favourites) with chequer patterns and conventional floral sprays. Massive at first, the construction became lighter as the evolution advanced, and in later specimens there is a tendency to florid enrichment; as in Fig. 9, where the back, cresting and framework are carved with a medley of foliated scrolls. There were local variations of the type, the treatment in Lancashire (Fig. 17) being particularly distinctive; while in Yorkshire and Derbyshire shortly before the Restoration another variety was introduced in which the space between the uprights is sometimes filled with arched members or an arcade decorated with small turned knobs.

Upholstered furniture was becoming plentiful in great houses about the end of Elizabeth I's reign. Chairs of X form continued to be made but are now very rare owing to the perishable nature of the beechwood frames. An arm-chair of this form, covered with faded velvet originally crimson and trimmed with tarnished gold fringe, once belonged to Archbishop Juxon, who, when Bishop of London, attended Charles I on the scaffold (Fig. 13). Among the magnificent furniture sold after the King's execution by the Council of State were a number of similar arm-chairs covered with velvet and cloth of silver, several being embroidered with the royal cognizances 'ye armes of England holden by beasts'.

In the early years of the seventeenth century, chairs with padded backs were made in sets without arms,[5] and were probably intended to accommodate the farthingale, or hooped skirt, which by then had attained extravagant dimensions. The Museum possesses two of these 'farthingale chairs', one still retaining its original covering (Fig. 12). Another early upholstered arm-chair is shown in Fig. 11. This is covered with velvet. At Knole Park, Sevenoaks, there are upholstered arm-chairs of far more elaborate character. Several are of X form and date from James I's reign, while others closely resemble French and Flemish examples and those represented in the engravings of domestic interiors by Abraham Bosse,[6] the arm-supports, legs and stretchers being completely covered with silk or velvet. Chairs in favour under the Protectorate seemed to reflect the austerity of the times, for their structure is frequently composed with plain bars, turned knobs, the seats and back panels being upholstered in cowhide fastened to the frame by brass-headed nails The chair shown in Fig. 14 is of a type completely alien to the English tradition. It was probably designed by Francis Cleyn, who was associated with the famous tapestry-works at Mortlake, and who favoured an Italo-Flemish style. Few chairs of this kind seem to have been made in England.

Soon after the return of Charles II and his court from exile the character of fashionable chairs was transformed, and a new type (already familiar in France and Holland) was introduced in which walnut was used in conjunction with caning for the first time. In early specimens the arms are flat and bowed, and uprights and stretchers are spirally turned, these members at the points of junction being morticed and tenoned into rectangular blocks (Fig. 21). Chairs of this kind, 'turned all over' and admirable from the functional point of view, were soon superseded by another variety of which the ornate baroque character aptly expresses the spirit of the age. Scrolled forms were employed for arms and front legs, stretchers, cresting and back panel framing being now exploited as decorative areas. These members were pierced and lavishly carved. A crown supported by *amorini* (appropriate to the restored monarchy) is among the most familiar motives, but the craftsmen's exuberant fancy was responsible for considerable variety in the ornament employed. In a fine arm-chair (Fig. 29) a crowned female head decorates front stretcher and cresting, while *amorini* sport amid grape-laden branches below. These late Stuart chairs in some instances closely approximate to Continental models, but in foreign examples the rope of the spiral turning is thicker, the hollows less prominent, the resulting twist being close and rapid. The ornament of imported chairs is generally more crisply cut, lighter in handling and in lower relief; while the stretcher between the back legs is often omitted. Beech stained to resemble walnut was employed for the cheaper varieties, though owing to its vulnerability to worm Evelyn would have liked to see its use prohibited.[7]

About 1690 a tendency becomes noticeable towards greater sobriety in design. The height of the back is increased, and throughout the structure there is a marked emphasis on vertical lines. The uprights and legs are of baluster form, and front stretcher and cresting are often composed of pierced scrolls symmetrically arranged. The ornate front stretcher was abandoned on certain models, and replaced by carved diagonal rails meeting in a central finial. As an alternative to carving, the space between the uprights was filled with pierced foliage and scrollwork. Some of these chairs, dating from William III's reign, recall designs by the celebrated Huguenot architect, Daniel Marot, who came over from Holland and spent several years here in the service of William III. In the attempt to produce a handsome chamber ornament rather than a serviceable seat sound principles of construction were sometimes sacrificed, socket and dowel being substituted for tenon and mortice as a means of attachment.

Many of these late Stuart chairs were japanned, a form of decoration for which at this period there was an avid demand. In a set of this kind at Ham House a naïve attempt has been made to reproduce an Oriental form. They bear the coronet of Elizabeth Dysart, Duchess of Lauderdale (Fig. 28) and are probably the set described in an inventory of 1683 as '12 back stooles with cane bottoms, japanned'. Decorated with birds, figures and floral sprays on a dark green ground, where the surface has not been exposed to the sun, the japanned ornament still retains its poly-chromatic brilliance. 'Cane chairs japanned' are often found entered in contemporary inventories, but on seat furniture such decoration was particularly perishable and very few genuine specimens have survived. It is probable that most chairs with cane seats were also furnished with loose squab-cushions. These have rarely survived.

In the upholstered chairs which became fashionable soon after the Restoration the framework was of turned walnut; the backs were low and the arms were padded on their upper surfaces. About the middle of the reign a more luxurious type of 'Easie' chair was introduced, embroideries of various kinds and figured Genoa velvets and damasks being employed for the coverings. In the Queen's Closet at Ham there are two winged chairs with iron ratchets to let down the backs which were made for the Duke and Duchess of Lauderdale, and are described in the 1679 inventory as 'two sleeping chayers carv'd and guilt frames covered with crimson and gould stuff'. The scrolled front stretchers centre in *amorini* holding a bunch of grapes and the front legs rest on sea-horses (Fig. 25). Ham is plentifully supplied with upholstered chairs of this period, all still retaining their original coverings, and a set (in the Withdrawing Room when the inventory was taken) is highly characteristic of the baroque splendours that caused the house equipped by Elizabeth Dysart to be regarded by contemporaries as a synonym for luxury (Fig. 24). The arms finish in dolphin's heads, and the legs and stretchers are carved with the interlaced bodies of the fish, gilding and colour being combined in the enrichment. In the inventory the set is described as consisting of '6 arm chairs, 6 back stools, carved and gilt covered with rich brocade'; and this red and yellow brocaded satin is largely responsible for the opulent effect. Here the fringes are straight, but on other easy chairs of the period such trimmings are tasselled and elaborately festooned.

The accounts of the Lord Chamberlain's Department and the Warrants issued by the Master of the Great Wardrobe throw valuable light on the evolution of style and on the activities of the craftsmen who made furniture for the Crown. At this time they afford some evidence of specialization. For example, in the output of Thomas Roberts, who supplied a quantity of fine furniture for Chatsworth and the Royal palaces under William III, chairs figure prominently, while early in George I's reign Richard Roberts, probably his son, is found describing himself as 'Chairmaker to His Majesty' (see Fig. 42).

The tendency towards more disciplined and restrained design becomes increasingly evident towards the century's close. In the new type of walnut chair introduced from Holland soon after 1700 the form, purged of redundant ornament, was based upon the principle of contrasted curves. English makers were quick to appreciate the opportunity which this curvilinear principle afforded: the imported models were freely adapted and in the process largely transformed. When the type becomes fully naturalized, a continuous rhythm pervades the structure and the proportions are so nicely adjusted that even minor variations would falsify the scale. The finer specimens of these so-called 'Queen Anne' chairs provide a remarkable instance of that newly awakened appreciation of form which manifests itself at this time throughout the whole decorative field. If the eighteenth century has strong claims to be regarded as the golden age of English craftsmanship, with the native tradition reinforced by the skilful assimilation of foreign techniques, we may well be disposed to hold that chairmakers at least never surpassed their achievements of the early decades.

At first, slightly curved uprights enclose a wide splat pierced and carved with foliated ornament, while the front legs are of cabriole[8] form ending in hoof or club feet and united by stretchers (Fig. 42). This form of leg, which had been gradually evolved, was the starting point of the whole development, the lines of the other members being made to conform. Later, the curve of the uprights becomes more pronounced; vase or fiddle splats follow the shape of the sitter's back; seat rails are rounded at the corners, and the legs, no longer united by stretchers, end in claw-and-ball feet—an Oriental motive of great antiquity now adopted as a favourite terminal. The splats, uprights and seat in chairs of high quality are veneered with figured burr walnut, while the more delicate carved ornament is applied (Fig. 54). Sometimes carving is replaced by marquetry decoration – the owner's crest amid mantling or a cypher and arabesques (Fig. 39). Japanned chairs were produced in large numbers and often figure in contemporary inventories and notices of sales. Many were imported from trading stations in China, being made from European models and lacquered in the East; but time has taken a heavy toll of them, and few examples, imported or indigenous, now survive (Fig. 40).

In upholstered chairs contemporary with the early curvilinear type, the cabriole form is adopted for the underframing, while for the coverings velvet, needlework, or tapestry was employed. Winged arm-chairs had been introduced toward the end of Charles II's reign, and the form soon became more or less standardized, the wings finishing in padded arm-rests with an outward curve. The Museum possesses a well-known example of these 'Easie', or so-called 'Grandfather' chairs, covered with the original needlework, which in this instance is of exceptional interest because the scenes are taken from plates in Ogilby's folio *Virgil* published in 1658 (Fig. 45).

After 1720 mahogany imported from the West Indies[9] began to be used for the manufacture of chairs on an extensive scale, gradually supplanting walnut as the fashionable wood. Many fine walnut chairs were, however, made down to the middle of the eighteenth century. The influence of this new material, hard and close-grained, and lending itself admirably to the purposes of the carver[10] is observable both in the design and decoration of chairs – the nature of the material always goes far to determine the design, to which ornament in its turn is inseparably related. With the introduction of mahogany there was a revulsion from dignified simplicity and a renewed demand for lavish enrichment. This change of taste, which declares itself unmistakably soon after the death of Queen Anne, inaugurates the second phase of the English baroque style, in which ornate splendour sometimes comes perilously near to vulgarity. Nothing is more characteristic than the ostentatious furniture decorated with animal and human motives which was fashionable early in George II's reign: essentially plastic in conception, it found an ideally suitable environment in the palatial Palladian houses of that magnificent age.

In the upholstered chairs with low backs and wide seats made to accommodate full-bottomed coats and wide hooped-skirts the favourite lion motive was frequently employed: the head mask and paws, even the shaggy mane and hocks of the animal, constitute the salient ornament – realistically rendered and vigorously carved. Many of these chairs were gilded to match the monumental side-tables in saloons, and among the finest are those designed by William Kent for Sir Robert Walpole at Houghton Hall. The head and claws of an eagle were sometimes substituted as terminals (Fig. 52), and in the use of such motives (which have a pedigree dating back to the early French Renaissance) no consistency was attempted: while the arms end in lions' heads, a female mask may decorate the knees. This grandiose baroque style is well represented by the unusual arm-chair (shown in Fig. 58) with its vigorously modelled legs, enriched with masks carved in high relief.

Among the specialized varieties dating from the early years of the century are chairs made for reading or writing in a library. The occupant sat astride, resting his arms on the padded supports, with a book or writing material on the desk attached to the back (Fig. 51). The stretchers on this example are an old-fashioned feature which must here have been retained in order to strengthen this essentially practical piece of furniture.

About 1740 the influence of the French *Rococo* style becomes discernible in the design and decoration of fashionable chairs, and baroque solidity is gradually superseded by lighter forms, rhythmical lines and delicate ornament in low relief. The solid splat is pierced and carved with scrolls and foliage (Fig. 60); the line of the uprights becomes almost vertical, tapering upwards to meet the top rail which rises into a 'cupid's bow' cresting; the seat rail is no longer rounded at the corners, and as an alternative to the cabriole, the straight leg united by stretchers is employed (Fig. 67). In the following decade the rococo flood set in strongly (e.g. Figs. 64 and 70),[11] fed by the tributary streams of the Gothic (Fig. 81) and Chinese (Fig. 77). Though the craze for these pseudo-medieval and Oriental motives was a comparatively ephemeral vogue, it served to provide a wide repertory of ornament, which together with the makers' remarkable fertility of invention goes far to account for the extraordinary variety in the design of contemporary chairs. Another factor helps to explain this variety: patterns from now onward were widely disseminated through the publication of illustrated trade pattern-books. Of these, of course, Chippendale's *Director* (1st edition 1754) is by far the best known,[12] and in the ample selection of chairs there provided, free adaptations of French models (Fig. 64) are combined with excursions into the Chinese and Gothic styles. Relatively few chairs in the mid-eighteenth century can be traced to any particular pattern-book,[13] but the backs of a set (Fig. 68) in the Macquoid Bequest correspond with one of Chippendale's designs.[14] The fullest expression of rococo caprice is represented by chairs in which the splats are formed of interlaced ribbons realistically carved – a conceit which certainly violates functional propriety, however remarkable as a technical *tour de force*. Chippendale observes that 'several sets have been made which have given entire satisfaction', and four chairs of very high quality from such a set are remarkably close to a plate in the *Director* (1st edition, Pl. XVI) (Fig. 70). Here the legs end in scroll feet, a form of terminal borrowed from France and adapted as an alternative to the claw-and-ball.[15]

Grotesque travesties of Gothic ornament may be found in some contemporary patterns, and though Horace Walpole and a small circle of like-minded enthusiasts with a relish for the 'true Gothic' affected to disdain such attempts of ignorant cabinet-makers, their own ventures of this kind were scarcely less absurd. The more extravagant flights of fancy were 'unrealizable aspirations', and in general the characteristic motives were used only as a variant of the rococo, cusping and tracery being confined to the splat. The Chinese 'taste', on the other hand, has distinct claims to be regarded as an independent decorative convention – even perhaps as a definite style (e.g. Fig. 78).

While the fashion for 'Indian goods' of all kinds was, of course, of long standing, its inception dating back to the Elizabethan age, the late Stuart imitations were confined to surface decoration and, save in rare instances,[16] did not affect the structural form. With the revival of the taste just before the middle of the century there was an attempt to reproduce Oriental types – or rather to produce something that would pass as Chinese among those who had no first-hand acquaintance with the East. Sir William Chambers in his *Designs of Chinese Buildings, Furniture, etc.*, 1757, gave two drawings from Chinese chairs,[17] but authentic models were not calculated to appeal to such fashionable designers as Chippendale, Darly and Halfpenny,[18] who for some years had been among the leading exponents of the vogue. It was far more consistently exploited than the Gothic for chairs. Backs and arms were filled with 'Chinese railing': pagoda ornament being often introduced; seat rails were decorated with frets, and though the legs were generally quadrilateral, there are examples in which they are turned to imitate bamboo. Sometimes the Chinese motives were used merely as a flavouring and combined with rococo detail with charming effect: there may be a central splat formed of scrolls and foliage, while the treatment of the legs and pierced stretchers is resolutely 'Chinese'. At this time it was usual for one or more rooms in large houses to be furnished throughout in this pseudo-Oriental taste: in such apartments all was made to conform to the prevailing vogue, and the chairs were japanned to harmonize with the rest of the contents. Chippendale observes of his designs for such chairs in the *Director* that they are 'very proper for a Lady's Dressing-Room especially if it is hung with India paper'.

Standing somewhat apart from the main evolution are the 'Windsor chairs', the most conspicuous of rustic varieties, produced from the end of the seventeenth century onwards amid the beechwoods of the Chilterns with High Wycombe as the centre. The salient characteristics of this type are the bent-wood bars, forming arms, backs and stretchers, and the use of dowel joints at the points of junction. In some examples the top-rail is shaped and supported on spindles with or without a central splat which is often pierced with a star, the Prince of Wales's plume, or other ornament; but the hooped back is a more familiar form. The seat is nearly always of elm, the bent members of ash or yew, the turned legs and spindles normally of beech. Windsor chairs were not confined to cottages and farmhouses: painted green, red or yellow they were frequently used in tea-gardens, and places of public resort, and were even to be found in lavishly furnished houses. The influence of contemporary fashion can be traced in details of the design – for instance in the Gothic variety, which may be regarded as the aristocrats of the type (Fig. 80). Here, spindles are replaced by a series of splats pierced with cusped tracery and contained within a pointed arch, the front legs of cabriole shape replacing the ordinary turned supports. Windsor chairs have never been superseded, and in the manufacture traditional patterns are still retained.

Among other specialized varieties are chairs introduced early in the eighteenth century for halls and corridors. In the 3rd edition of the *Director*, 1762, Chippendale illustrates six designs and states that 'they may be made of mahogany or any other wood, and painted'. Often the arms and crest of the owner were painted in the centre of the back. Porters, who had to wait in draughty halls, were also sometimes provided with hooded chairs specially suited for the purpose. Arm-chairs of exceptional size were also made in successive styles for the Masters of City Companies and Presidents of Freemasons' Lodges, the arms of the Company, or some symbolic device, figuring in many instances in the decoration (Figs. 63 and 84).

Soon after the accession of George III a new and powerful impetus transformed the character of fashionable furniture. The 3rd edition of Chippendale's *Director*, 1762, is devoted entirely to the rococo and its derivatives, but the period of indulgence in caprice and fancy was rapidly approaching its end. Robert Adam, after a long study of classical design and ornament in Italy and Dalmatia, had returned home and already become prominent as an architect. In 1761 he had drawn out plans for providing the Duke of Northumberland with a suite of rooms at Syon which was to be 'entirely in the Antique Style' – a date which may be taken to inaugurate the classical revival. Soon furniture and the whole range of domestic equipment manifested 'the electric power of this revolution in art', though the transformation was not suddenly effected, and the introduction of classical motives in the decoration preceded any far-reaching structural change. An important example of this transitional phase is a gilded arm-chair (Fig. 83), one of a set formerly at 19 Arlington Street, which was designed by Adam in 1764 and made by Thomas Chippendale for Sir Lawrence Dundas. It retains the curvilinear form of 'French' rococo chairs but is carved with sphinxes and other classical motives. After the style had become fully established, Adam's ceremonial chairs for drawing-rooms and saloons corresponded closely with French models, though the ornament is generally larger in scale. They were made of beech, or another soft wood, with the frame-work moulded and entirely gilded. The legs are tapered, or turned and fluted, and curved supports spring from cappings at the corners of the seat-rail to meet the bowed arms. Fine examples of these ceremonial chairs may still be seen at

Osterly (Fig. 94), and other great houses for which Adam was responsible.

The mahogany chairs of the classical revival afford a marked contrast to those in the rococo style. Once again, as in the early years of the century, the architect intervened (and on a more comprehensive scale) to determine the forms of furniture which were to accord with his decorative schemes. Symmetrical curves and studied proportions were now preferred to florid enrichment, and the carved or inlaid ornament drawn from the classical repertory of motives – husks, honeysuckle, wheat-ears, paterae and urns – was employed with an admirable sense of fitness and carefully related to the structural lines. The extent of the transformation can readily be appreciated if specimens of rococo and neo-classical chairs are compared (Figs. 75 and 89): it will be seen that they represent fundamentally different and conflicting ideals.

Horace Walpole, visiting Osterley in 1773, notes[19] that 'the chairs are taken from antique lyres and make charming harmony'. Three large sets show with what resource a first-rate designer could adapt and vary this familiar classical form (Figs. 86, 87 and 88). These chairs are veritable masterpieces of craftsmanship and in the pristine state in which they were delivered to the house. Another arm-chair (Fig. 99) is from a set in a room at Osterley decorated and furnished in the 'Etruscan' taste, and corresponds closely with a drawing in the Soane Museum dated 6 March 1776. Adam observes in the *Works in Architecture* that 'a mode of decoration has been here attempted which differs from any hitherto practiced in Europe'. He confesses that ancient and modern authorities have failed to yield him any information concerning the interior decoration of the Etruscans, and explains that 'the style of the ornament and colouring' are imitated from vases and urns. He enriched the low-toned palette of terracottas, yellows and browns with a judicious admixture of lighter hues. Delicate, slightly bizarre and small in scale, suited only to relatively confined spaces, Etruscan painting on walls and furniture never obtained an extensive vogue. In these Osterley chairs and in other fine examples of the style in its early phase, the backs are hooped or rectilinear; but oval, heart and shield-shaped backs soon became fashionable, slender curved ribs carved with paterae or festoons of drapery sometimes replacing the central splat (Figs. 93–97).

In trade publications of this period the style is seen translated into vernacular terms, purged of much of the classical character that fitted it for 'the parade of life' and skilfully adapted to domestic use. A wide selection of patterns is represented, yet they do not amount to a tithe of the variety found in the contemporary chairs that still survive; for the classic formula in the later phases of the style was so freely interpreted that it imposed no severe restraint on the designer's fancy. The terms 'Hepplewhite' and 'Sheraton' are to be understood in a generic sense: many of the finest examples of the period bear no more than a general resemblance to illustrations in their books; none can be assigned to them on documentary grounds. Heart and shield shapes are particularly associated with Hepplewhite and Fig. 103 shows a chair which corresponds closely with a design in the *Guide*, 1st edition, 1788 (Pl. 4); but he was certainly not responsible for introducing these shapes.

His avowed aim was 'to exhibit the present taste' omitting such articles as were 'the production of whim at the instance of caprice'. In the first edition, 1788, cabriole legs of attenuated form are still retained for chairs of state, and the scrolled 'French foot' (favoured by Chippendale in the *Director*) is recommended as a terminal for seats of this kind. Hepplewhite draws attention to the concave shaping of the back, 'the bars and frame sunk in a hollow, or rising in a round projection with a band of list on the inner and outer edges' – technical refinements which may be seen on many contemporary examples. In the Preface he observes that 'a new and very elegant fashion has arisen within these few years' of finishing chairs with japanned decoration: this treatment allowed of a variety of grounds, so that seat furniture thus treated could be made to harmonize with the general colour-scheme of the room; while it had the further advantage that the framework might be 'less massy than is requisite for mahogany'. For decoration, floral garlands, sprays and medallions, painted in natural colours or grisaille, were employed. Hepplewhite's claim to have introduced the three feathers as an ornament is not established, for as the badge of the Prince of Wales's party it was in great request at the time. He illustrates an upholstered chair thus ornamented and with arms set 'much higher than usual' which he says 'has been executed with good effect for his Royal Highness the Prince of Wales' – not necessarily by Hepplewhite's firm (Fig. 93).

Explicit directions are given on the subject of upholstery. For japanned chairs with caned bottoms, cushions covered with linen are favoured to accord with the general hue: the strong and serviceable chairs made for dining-rooms should have 'seats of horse hair, plain, striped, chequered etc., at pleasure'; while for upholstered chairs with square backs (shown in the third edition, 1794) seats of red or blue morocco leather tied down with silk tassels are recommended. In this 'more elegant kind' medallions of printed or painted silk are to be inserted in the middle of the top rail.

Though Sheraton admits that he went the round of the shops and the selection of chairs in the *Drawing Book* (published in parts 1791–94) may be in a measure derived from the fashionable models in use, he had greater fertility of invention than Hepplewhite; and late eighteenth-century pseudo-classicism – now tending to an extreme of feminine elegance – is seen at its best in the designs for chairs, as for other varieties of furniture in his book. The majority of the backs are rectilinear; and the central splat, which retains scarcely a trace of true classic feeling, is flanked in some instances by carved and moulded bars (Fig. 105). These patterns for

'Parlour chairs' convey a suggestion of perilous fragility – combined in the best examples with impeccable craftsmanship and a most discriminating selection of woods. Three designs are given for upholstered chairs to be used in drawing-rooms, which are to be 'finished in white and gold, or the ornaments may be japanned'. The tablets in the centre of the deep-shaped seat rail are 'on French silk or satin, sewn on to the stuffing with borders round them', and seats and backs are to be decorated in the same style. Sheraton observes that 'chairs of this kind have an effect which far exceeds any conception we can have of them from an uncoloured engraving or even of a coloured one'; but examples made from these patterns and still retaining their original upholstery do not appear to survive. Chintz 'which may now be had of various patterns on purpose for chair seats', is also recommended for the drawing-room variety. Some designs are specially indicated as 'suitable for japanning', and the explanatory notes show that the most fanciful models were intended for this treatment; they could also be made in mahogany, and directions are given by which their ornate character might be suitably 'retrenched'. Few chairs of this time were made of satinwood, probably because for seat furniture it was thought to be too aggressive in tone, but Fig. 104, one of these comparatively rare examples, is of exceptional interest because it corresponds with the arm-chairs in a large set made by the firm of Seddon for Hauteville House, Guernsey, in 1790. 'Chair-making', writes Sheraton in his *Cabinet Dictionary*, 1803, 'is a branch generally confined to itself; as those who professedly work at it seldom engage to make cabinet furniture'. He adds that 'It is very remarkable, the difference of some chairs of precisely the same pattern, when executed by different chair-makers, arising chiefly from the want of taste concerning the beauty of an outline, of which we judge by the eye, more than the rigid rules of perspective'. In this judging by the eye – an incommunicable faculty which defies analysis – lies the secret of the singular excellence of line and proportion that distinguishes so many late eighteenth-century chairs.

The Regency Style – miscalled, since George, Prince of Wales became Regent in 1811, and the term in this context is commonly understood to cover the period 1800–20 – was highly eclectic in character, 'a medley or hotch-potch of all styles'. The Roman, the Greek, the Egyptian, the Gothic, the Chinese, even the Etruscan and the Moresque, each con-tributed their quota to the mixture; though several of these were minor fashions, tributaries of the main stream, and by the straiter sect 'Grecian severity' was consistently advocated as the ideal. This was 'a more intense and archaeological' classical revival, drawing its inspiration from a variety of sources in the ancient world. At the outset it owed something to the French *Directoire* style as interpreted by Henry Holland, and, had he lived, the English version of Empire might have been closer to its proto-type; for he was a designer of genius with Gallican enthusiasms. But Holland died in 1806 when the 'Regency' was still in the initial stage, and his brilliant gifts as a decorative artist (of which Southhill in Bedfordshire and the salvage from Carlton House at Buckingham Palace constitute the most impressive reminders) exercised little influence on the later phase. In its maturity Regency was a style in which 'breadth and repose of surface, that distinctness and contrast of outline that opposition of plain and enriched parts'[20] – in short, a reliance on formal excellence, simplicity, solidity and sound use of material constitute the strongest appeal. Chairs are not among the varieties of furniture in which these qualities are most prominently displayed. None the less a resolute attempt was made by the more erudite designers to ensure that they should conform to the new standards of orthodoxy: they were to reproduce as closely as possible the classic originals drawn by the protagonists of the movement on their travels abroad from bas-reliefs, vase-paintings and excavated remains (Fig. 110). This aspiration was imperfectly realized. Thomas Hope, the most learned of the group, might write (in 1807) that the 'pure taste of the antique reproduction of Greek forms for chairs, etc.' had been restored; but he was powerless to restrain the later makers of trade-catalogues in whose publications the classical originals were not only adapted to contemporary domestic use – 'taking not so much the mere pattern or imitation, but the spirit and principle on which the original was composed,'[21] but in some instances outrageously travestied as well.

By the votaries of the new cult of antiquity the models for chairs provided by the earlier neo-classical revival were regarded as hopelessly obsolete, and soon far-reaching changes affected the form. There is a marked emphasis on horizontal lines, and prominent features are the curved or 'sabre'-shaped front legs, the arms set high on the back uprights giving 'a characteristic high-shouldered appearance'; the top rail swept backwards and forming a continuous curve with the rear legs. 'Parlour chairs' were made of mahogany or rosewood inlaid with foliated patterns and stringing lines of brass (Fig. 114): many were japanned (for the fashion still persisted), classical motives in the decoration tending to supplant the naturalistic detail hitherto in vogue. In the more ambitious specimens the 'archaeological' bias of the movement is plainly declared. Thomas Hope recommends antique heads of 'helmeted warriors, winged figures emblematical of freedom, and lances surmounted by a Phrygian Cap of Liberty' as suitable ornaments for chairs; while archaic lions, gryphons, sphinxes, owls and winged female terminals (Fig. 112) were also included in what, with the increasing mania for symbolism,[22] became a veritable menagerie of animal forms. The arm-chair (Fig. 109) is of exceptional interest because it closely corresponds with a design dated 1804 and published by George Smith in his *Household Furniture* (Plate 56). The types for dining-room and parlour tended towards standardization, and it was into the arms and legs of drawing-room chairs that these 'heads of various animals' were introduced – a practice sanctioned by French precedent for which in the later phases of the movement an almost superstitious reverence was shown. Other Regency varieties – bergère, 'conversation' and 'hunting chairs' are not yet represented in the Museum collections.

Sheraton in his *Encyclopaedia*, 1807, observes that in chair-making 'it is extremely difficult to attain to anything really novel', and recommends those who are avid for novelties to sit down and see what they can do in that way themselves. This complaint, a confession of bankrupt invention, is echoed by later designers, and in pattern books published in the twenties there is a reversion to earlier forms, suggesting that many extant examples are often dated some years before they were made. The Regency style proved to be endowed with surprising vitality, and, albeit in an increasingly heavy and plain form, remained a living style until the 1860s, used mostly by conservative designers and cabinet-makers. However this 'Grecian' style, as it was called, attracted less attention than the more original inventions of the early Victorian era. Of these the 'Gothic' style, although it had rococo and regency antecedents, became increasingly 'archaeological' in character under the influence of the Catholic architect, designer and propagandist, A. W. N. Pugin (1812–52). At the same time the Louis XV style enjoyed a revival; inaccurately known as 'Louis XIV' it was eminently suited to the drawing room and a spate of light and elegant chairs, often painted and gilt, were produced (Fig. 115). The 'naturalistic' style, an original Victorian invention, used the flowing curves of the 'Louis XIV' style but combined them with naturalistic carving and decorative motives borrowed from other styles. Although disapproved of by contemporary critics who disliked its lack of historicism and called it 'nameless', the 'naturalistic' style was the vehicle for many innovations, including the Victorian classic, the balloon-back chair, and infinite varieties of luxuriantly upholstered arm-chairs and sofas. The 'Elizabethan' style, in contrast, was respectably based on historical English examples; nor did it suffer from the tractarian and Catholic overtones inherent in the Gothic style. The 'Elizabethan' chair (Fig. 118), based in fact on turned and carved late seventeenth-century examples, almost equalled the balloon-back in popularity.

In the 1860s several reformers, most notably William Morris (1834–96), made an attempt to create furnishings based on a close relationship between craftsman and designer and to bring artistic furniture into the houses of the masses. Morris & Co's turned wood chairs (Fig. 122), based on traditional country-made models, were among the few successes of this experiment. Morris, himself, was never active as a furniture designer but had great influence on the thinking and practice of most reformers. Among these were the architect E. W. Godwin (1833–86) and the designer B. J. Talbert (1838–81); the former designed furniture of startling originality based on Japanese and Greek designs, while the latter helped successfully to commercialize the 'reformed Gothic' of Morris, Burges and others. The Arts and Crafts Movement and the concept of 'Art

Furniture' arose directly from Morris's influence and the idiosyncratic
Art Nouveau chairs of the Glasgow architect C. R. Mackintosh (1868–
1928) and the more commercial products of William Birch & Co. of
High Wycombe are ultimately derived from his ideas. A more direct
link with Morris at the turn of the century is to be found in the work of
Ernest Gimson (1864–1919), who also based his chairs on traditional
models (Fig. 127). Victorian craftsmen and manufacturers were also
skilful at introducing new materials into chair manufacture; this selection,
however, can give only a hint of the immense variety of technique and
form apparent in their productions.

REFERENCES AND NOTES

(1) In the Royal Writs issued under Henry III ordering furniture for the King's private apartments, chairs are among the objects specified; a movable chair (*cathedra mobilis*) is mentioned.

(2) Though in the capital and a few provincial cities, such as Chester and York, guild regulations were rigidly enforced, they did not apply in country districts. Under James I the Shuttleworths of Gawthorpe employed a 'dish-thrower' to make them a 'thrown chair'. (Shuttleworth Accounts. Chetham Society. Vol. 35, p. 160.)

(3) Now exhibited in Room I.

(4) For evidence that chairs of this type were made for the Crown by Coffermakers and that their production was a specialized craft, see R. W. Symonds 'The Craft of the Coffermaker', *Connoisseur*, March 1941.

(5) In Elizabethan inventories of great houses, upholstered chairs, apparently made in sets, are listed and are sometimes described as covered 'suteable' (or to match) a bed.

(6) A French engraver, 1602–76.

(7) *Sylva*, 1st edition, 1664.

(8) The term is now used to denote 'a form of leg which curves outward . . . and then descends in a tapering reverse curve terminating in an ornamental foot' (Webster). In this sense it has no contemporary authority. In Hepplewhite's *Guide*, 1788, it is used to describe a variety of chair with a 'stuffed' back.

(9) Early importations of so-called 'Spanish mahogany' were obtained mainly from the West Indies, notably from Jamaica and Cuba and the Spanish Mainland; while the later and inferior variety came from Honduras in Central America.

(10) The surfaces of chairs were no longer veneered.

(11) But the rococo was never exploited in the most advanced degree on chairs, as it was, for example, on contemporary picture frames.

(12) Darly's *New Book of Chinese, Gothic and Modern Chairs*, 1752, is the only considerable work published before the *Director* which aimed at providing assistance to the trade.

(13) The most important in this connection are Ince and Mayhew's *Universal System of Household Furniture*, 1759–62, where some of the designs are obvious plagiarisms from *Director* plates, Manwaring's *The Cabinet and Chair Makers' Real Friend and Companion*, 1765, and *The Chair Makers' Guide*, 1766 – the last two intended for those who specialized in chairs.

(14) *Director*, 1st edition, Pl. XII. Though there is a strong probability that these and certain other chairs, which closely follow a design in the *Director*, were made by Chippendale's firm, only a bill could afford positive proof.

(15) In the *Director* there is only one design showing the claw-and-ball (3rd edition, Pl. XVIII, right).

(16) E.g. the japanned chairs in the Blue Drawing-room at Ham, Fig. 28.

(17) He notes that they are among the 'movables of the saloon' and are 'made sometimes of rosewood, ebony or lacquered work, and sometimes of bamboo'.

(18) William Halfpenny's *New Designs for Chinese Buildings*, 1750, in which a few designs for chairs are given, is the earliest publication of the kind, but the author states that the 'Chinese manner' had been 'already introduced here with success'.

(19) In a letter to the Countess of Upper Ossory, 21 June 1773.

(20) Hope, *Household Furniture*, 1807, p. 2.

(21) George Smith, *Household Furniture*, 1808. Preface p. vi.

(22) This aspect of the style is extremely prominent in the later trade catalogues, e.g. Richard Brown's *Rudiments of Drawing Cabinet and Upholstery Furniture*, 1822. Though Brown is perhaps the worst offender in the matter of symbolism, he rebukes makers who 'for the sake of notoriety' talk of Trafalgar Chairs and Waterloo feet.

SELECT BIBLIOGRAPHY

MACQUOID, P., and EDWARDS, R. *The Dictionary of English Furniture*. 3 vols. London, 1924–27. 2nd ed. 1954.

EDWARDS, R. *The Shorter Dictionary of English Furniture*. London, 1964.

GLOAG, J. *The Englishmans Chair*. London, 1964.

JOY, E. T. *The 'Country Life' Book of Chairs*. London, 1967.

VICTORIA AND ALBERT MUSEUM. WARD-JACKSON, P. *English Furniture Designs of the Eighteenth Century*. London, 1958.

COLERIDGE, A. *Chippendale Furniture*. London, 1968.

ASLIN, E. *Nineteenth Century English Furniture*. London, 1962.

SYMONDS, R. W., and WHINERAY, B. B. *Victorian Furniture*. London, 1962.

List of Illustrations

11 ARM-CHAIR. Wood, painted and gilded on a gesso ground. Covered with a plain red velvet. First quarter of the 17th century. H. 3 ft. 3 in., W. 2 ft. 3½ in.   W.58–1953

12 CHAIR. ('Farthingale type.') Oak; upholstered later in 'Turkey Work'. Second quarter of the 17th century. H. 3 ft. 1 in., W. 1 ft. 7 in. *Bequeathed by Col. G. B. Croft-Lyons.*   W.63–1926

13 ARM-CHAIR AND FOOTSTOOL. Beechwood; upholstered in velvet (originally crimson), trimmed with galloon, fringed, and studded with brass-headed nails. Formerly in the possession of William Juxon (d. 1663), Archbishop of Canterbury, at Little Compton Manor House, near Moreton-in-Marsh, Gloucestershire. The fact that Juxon attended Charles I on the scaffold gave rise to the long-standing, but probably erroneous, belief that it is the chair in which Charles I sat at his trial in Westminster Hall. Second quarter of the 17th century. H. 4 ft. 2 in., W. 2 ft. 9 in. Footstool. D. 1 ft. 7¾ in., W. 1 ft. 9¾ in. *Bought with the aid of a grant from the National Art-Collections Fund.*   W.12 and 13–1928

14 CHAIR. Carved wood, formerly gilded. Similar to a set originally at Holland House, Kensington, designed by Francis Cleyn, an artist-decorator famous for his association with the Mortlake tapestry workshops. Second quarter of the 17th century. H. 3 ft. 7½ in., W. 2 ft. 3¼ in.   W.9–1953

15 ARM-CHAIR. Oak. Back and seat covered with knotted woollen pile ('Turkey Work'). From Beau Desert, Warwickshire. Second quarter of the 17th century. H. 3 ft. 2 in., W. 2 ft. 4 in.   W.30–1923

16 ARM-CHAIR. Oak, the back panel carved with a vase and conventional foliage. Lancashire type. About 1640. H. 3 ft. 8 in., W. 2 ft.   W.33–1938

17 CHAIR. Carved and turned oak. Lancashire type. Dated 1641. H. 3 ft. 10 in., W. 1 ft. 10 in.   W.10–1947

18 CHAIR-TABLE. Carved oak with applied ornament. The back, revolving on pins, tips forward to form a table. About 1650–60. H. 4 ft. 5 in., W. 2 ft. 2 in.   W.45–1948

19 CHAIR. Oak covered with leather studded with brass-headed nails. The front legs and stretcher of knob-turning. About 1660. H. 2 ft. 11 in., W. 1 ft. 7 in.   W.9–1923

20 CHAIR. Turned walnut upholstered in tent-stich embroidery. The arms of Hill of Spaxton Yarde and Pounsford, Somerset, impaling Gurdon of Assington Hall, Suffolk, and Letton, Norfolk, relate to the marriage in 1641 of Roger Hill of Pounsford (d. 29th June 1655) with his second wife Abigail (d. 3rd December 1658), born Gurdon. From Denham Place, Buckinghamshire. The embroidery between 1641–55; the frame about 1660. H. 3 ft. 1 in., W. 1 ft. 8½ in.   W.124–1937

21 ARM-CHAIR. Walnut spirally turned; caned seat and back. About 1660. H. 3 ft. 5 in., W. 2 ft. 2 in.   W.64–1911

22 CHAIR. Oak covered with leather studded with brass-headed nails. The carved stretcher resembles those on early Post-Restoration walnut chairs. About 1670. H. 3 ft. 2¾ in., W. 1 ft. 6½ in.   94–1893

23 ARM-CHAIR. Walnut, turned and carved, with gilded enrichments. At Ham House, Petersham. About 1675. H. 3 ft. 8½ in., W. 2 ft. 1 in.   H.H.35–1948

24 ARM-CHAIR. Carved with dolphin motives, painted and gilded. Covered with the original crimson brocaded satin. At Ham House, Petersham. One of a set of twelve described in an inventory dated 1679. About 1675. H. 3 ft. 3½ in., W. 2 ft. 1 in.   H.H.81–1948

25 'SLEEPING-CHAIR.' Carved and gilded with adjustable back. Covered with the original crimson brocade matching the wall-hangings. One of a pair at Ham House, Petersham. Described in an inventory made for the Duke of Lauderdale in 1679 (the approximate date of the chairs). H. 4 ft. 3½ in., W. 2 ft. 5½ in.   H.H.141–1948

26 ARM-CHAIR. Carved walnut, upholstered in black leather, with an iron ratchet for adjusting the back. About 1680. H. 3 ft. 11¾ in. W. 2 ft. 3 in.
W.40–1927

27 ARM-CHAIR. Carved and gilded wood, covered with green velvet. About 1680. H. 3 ft. 7 in., W. 2 ft. 2 in. *Given by the seventh Duke of Buccleuch.*
W.32–1918

28 CHAIR. Wood japanned in polychrome on a black ground with oriental motives. The cresting bears the cipher and coronet of Elizabeth Dysart, Duchess of Lauderdale. One of a set at Ham House, Petersham, probably that described in an inventory dated 1683 as '12 back stooles with cane bottoms, japanned'. An early and naïve attempt to imitate an Oriental form. About 1680. H. 4 ft. 2½ in., W. 1 ft. 8½ in.   H.H.115–1948

29 ARM-CHAIR. Carved and turned walnut with cane back and seat. About 1680. H. 4 ft. 3 in., W. 2 ft. *Given by Sir George Donaldson.*   W.145–1919

30 ARM-CHAIR. Carved walnut. Cane seat and back. 1685. H. 4 ft. 6½ in., W. 2 ft. 4½ in. Given by Mr E. Bullivant.   W.16–1955

31 ARM-CHAIR. Carved beechwood. Embroidered seat and back. From Drayton House, Northamptonshire. About 1685. H. 4 ft., W. 2 ft. 4 in.
W.34–1950

32 ARM-CHAIR. Beechwood painted black and partly gilded. Covered with original yellow satin decorated with couched red cord, a rare form of late 17th century upholstery. One of a set at Ham House, Petersham. About 1675. H. 3 ft. 8½ in., W. 2 ft. 3½ in.   H.H.152–1948

33 CHAIR. Beechwood, carved and painted black. The embroidery appears to be of later date. Originally the chair probably had a cane seat. H. 4 ft. 4½ in., W. 1 ft. 8½ in. About 1690. *Given by Mr Frank Green.*   W.37–1916

34 CHAIR. Carved walnut. Cane back; seat upholstered in green velvet. About 1690. From the Mulliner Collection. H. 4 ft. 7 in., W. 1 ft. 6 in. *Given by Mr R. Freeman Smith.*   W.31–1925

35 CHAIR. Carved and painted beechwood. About 1695. H. 4 ft. 3½ in., W. 1 ft. 6½ in.   W.71–1911

36 SETTEE. Carved walnut; upholstered in cross-stich embroidery. Formerly in the possession of Thomas Coningsby (d. 1729), 1st Earl of Coningsby,

at Hampton Court, Herefordshire. About 1700. H. 4 ft. 6¼ in., W. 5 ft. 2 in. *Bought from the funds of the Bryan Bequest.* W.15–1945

37 CHAIR. Carved walnut. Embroidered seat and back. About 1700. H. 3 ft. 11 in., W. 1 ft. 10 in. *Given by Mr Francis Mallett in commemoration of the twenty-fifth anniversary of the National Art-Collections Fund.* W.45–1928

38 CHAIR (one of three). Walnut, upholstered in modern woollen plush. About 1700. H. 3 ft. 1½ in., W. 1 ft. 9 in. *Given by Mr Douglas Eyre in memory of his father and mother.* W.27–1922

39 CHAIR. Walnut with marquetry decoration which includes the initials 'W.R.', crowned. Re-covered with a velvet of the period; the original covering was of red velvet. About 1710. H. 3 ft. 7 in., W. 1 ft. 9½ in.

W.38–1929

40 CHAIR. Beechwood, japanned green and gold on a red ground. About 1710. H. 3 ft. 9 in., W. 1 ft. 10 in. W.44–1938

41 CHAIR. Carved and gilded gesso, with upholstery in crimson and gold figured velvet. A similar velvet, ordered from John Johnson & Co., Mercers, in July 1714, covers Queen Anne's bed and the accompanying chairs and stools at Hampton Court Palace. About 1715. H. 3 ft. 3¾ in., W. 2 ft. 0½ in.

W.15–1931

42 CHAIR. Carved walnut, upholstered in green velvet. Style of Daniel Marot. A set of eighteen similar chairs at Hampton Court Palace were supplied by Richard Roberts, Chairmaker to George I, in 1717, and in the receipt are described as having 'India backs', presumably in reference to the pierced carving. H. 3 ft. 10 in., W. 1 ft. 9¾ in. W.28–1909

43 CHAIR. Beechwood. Carved and gilded gesso. Upholstered in red and gold cut velvet of the early 18th century. Cresting carved with the arms (*sable three nags' heads erased argent*) granted in April 1717 to Sir William Humphreys, Bart., Lord Mayor of London, 1714–15. About 1717. H. 4 ft., W. 2 ft. 0½ in. W.62–1935

44 CHAIR. Veneered with walnut and with gilded details, covered with velvet which is apparently original. Believed to have come from Houghton Hall, Norfolk, where other chairs of an identical pattern are still preserved. The velvet on the Houghton chairs has a silver galloon trimming instead of nails. Second decade of the 18th century. H. 3 ft. 5 in., W. 2 ft. 1 in. W.15–1960

45 WING ARM-CHAIR. Walnut; upholstered in embroidery of coloured wools (*tent- and cross-stitch*) with eleven scenes after illustrations engraved by Wenceslaus Hollar and Pierre Lombart after Francis Cleyn, for the folio *Virgil,* edited and printed by John Ogilby (1600–76), London, 1658. About 1720. H. 3 ft. 11 in., W. 2 ft. 8 in. *Given by Douglas Eyre in memory of his father and mother.* W.25–1922

46 CHAIR. Turned and painted beech, upholstered in English tapestry work probably woven in London. One of a pair. About 1720. H. 3 ft. 9 in., W. 1 ft. 11½ in. *Given by Mr F. W. Green.* W.8–1932

47 CHAIR. Walnut, covered with embroidery (the fringe may be of later date). About 1720. H. 3 ft. 8¼ in., W. 1 ft. 10¼ in. *Given by Mr Frank Green.*

W.47–1916

48 CHAIR. Walnut, upholstered in *tent-stich* embroidery. About 1725. H. 3 ft. 3¼ in., W. 1 ft. 10¼ in. Seat cover restored. *Given by Mr Frank Green.*

W.34–1916

49 ARM-CHAIR. Carved walnut, upholstered in black leather. About 1720. H. 3 ft. 2 in., W. 2 ft. *Given by Brigadier W. E. Clark, C.M.G., D.S.O., through the National Art-Collections Fund.* W.12–1958

50 ARM-CHAIR ('Writing-Chair'). Carved walnut, the seat upholstered in velvet. The arms terminate in eagles' heads. About 1725. H. 2 ft. 9 in., W. 2 ft. 1 in. *Given by Mrs M. Marchant.* W.24–1924

51 READING AND WRITING CHAIR. Carved mahogany, upholstered in leather. About 1725. H. 2 ft. 9 in., W. 2 ft. 7 in. Shown with the hinged trays in the arms open. W.47–1948
Such chairs were used in libraries. Sheraton in his *Cabinet Dictionary*, 1803, illustrates a late variety and writes '. . . . the reader places himself with his back to the front of the chair, and rests his arms on the top yoke.'

52 ARM-CHAIR. Carved walnut, upholstered in red velvet. About 1725. H. 3 ft. 6 in., W. 2 ft. 8¾ in. *Given by the children of the late Sir George Donaldson in his memory.* W.38–1925
Eagles' heads and claws were sometimes adopted as terminals as an alternative to the favourite lion motives of the early Georgian period.

53 CHAIR. Walnut, carved and in part veneered. About 1725. H. 3 ft. 3 in., W. 1 ft. 9½ in. *Given by Sir Paul A. Makins, Bt.* W.37–1920

54 CHAIR. Walnut, carved and in part veneered. One of a set. About 1730–35. H. 3 ft. 4 in., W. 1 ft. 11 in. 680–1890

55 ARM-CHAIR. Carved rosewood inlaid with engraved brass, covered with contemporary embroidery. Similar to the style of John Channon. About 1740. H. 3 ft., W. 1 ft. 9 in. *Given by Brigadier W. E. Clark, C.M.G., D.S.O., through the National Art-Collections Fund.* W.32–1959

56 CHAIR. Walnut. The back and seat covered with a modern material. About 1730. H. 3 ft. 6 in., W. 1 ft. 11½ in. 235–1898

57 CHAIR. One of a pair. Carved mahogany covered with contemporary needlework. Originally from Copped Hall, Essex. About 1725–30. H. 3 ft. 7 in., L. 1 ft. 11½ in., D. 2 ft. 3½ in. *On loan from the Leicester Museum and Art Gallery.*

58 CHAIR. Carved mahogany, the back veneered, the arms terminating in lions' heads, the legs carved with lions' masks. About 1730. *Given by Mr F. H. Reed.* W.63–1953

59 CHAIR. Carved and gilded wood, one of a set at Ham House, Petersham. This chair, with its X-form legs, is strongly influenced by the style of William Kent. About 1725–30. H. 3 ft. 4½ in., W. 2 ft. 1 in. H.H.28–1948

60 CHAIR. Carved mahogany. One of a set. About 1740. In the centre of the splat the crest of Eyre. H. 3 ft. 2½ in., W. 2 ft. *Given by Mr Douglas Eyre.*

W.32–1922

61 CHAIR. Carved walnut, upholstered in modern damask. About 1745. H. 3 ft. 3 in., W. 1 ft. 11½ in. *Bequeathed by Mr C. W. Farwell.*

Circ. 294–1959

62 CHAIR. Walnut, upholstered in *tent-* and *cross-stitch* embroidery. Mid 18th century. H. 3 ft. 3 in., W. 1 ft. 7 in. *One of a set of six bequeathed by Lady W. S. Theobald.* W.19–1938

63 PRESIDENT'S CHAIR. Carved mahogany, with painted and gilded detail. Made for the President of Lyon's Inn, an Inn of Chancery, Newcastle Street, Strand. About 1750. H. 4 ft. 2 in., W. 2 ft. 9¼ in. W.63–1911
Large presidential chairs elaborately carved were made at this period for the City Companies, Masonic Lodges and the Inns of Court.

64 ARM-CHAIR. Carved mahogany, covered with contemporary needlework. the lower part of the front legs corresponds to that of a 'French Chair' in Chippendale's *Director*, 1754. There is a stool ensuite (W.39–1946). Mid 18th century. H. 3 ft. 7½ in., W. 2 ft. 2½ in. *Given by Brigadier W. E. Clark, C.M.G., D.S.O., through the National Art-Collections Fund.* W.16–1956

65 ARM-CHAIR. Carved and gilded wood upholstered with modern silk damask. The five different designs on the arms, front and legs suggest that this may have been a 'pattern chair'. About 1750. H. 3 ft. 9 in., W. 2 ft. W.5–1959

66 CHAIR. Carved mahogany, upholstered in modern silk damask. Mid 18th century. H. 3 ft. 1½ in., W. 2 ft. 2 in. *Given by Mr F. D. Lycett-Green.* W.42–1947

67 CHAIR. Carved mahogany, covered with modern velvet. Mid 18th century. H. 3 ft. 2 in., W. 1 ft. 11 in. *Given by Mr Frank Partridge.* W.2 1952

68 ARM-CHAIR. Carved mahogany, the seat upholstered in needlework of coloured silks and wools. Closely similar to a design dated 1753, Chippendale's *Director*, 1st edition, 1754, plate XII (3) and probably made by his firm (cf. No. 69). H. 3 ft. 1¾ in., W. 2 ft. 2½ in. *Macquoid Bequest.* W.46–1925

69 Design for a chair from Thomas Chippendale's *Director*, 1st edition, 1754, plate XII (cf. No. 68).

70 CHAIR. Carved mahogany with seat upholstered in contemporary needlework. The splat resembles designs for 'Ribband Back' chairs in Chippendale's *Director*, 1st edition, 1754, plate XVI. One of four. About 1755. H. 3 ft. 3½ in., W. 2 ft. 2 in. *Clarke Bequest.* W.65–1935

71 CHAIR. Carved mahogany. One of a pair. About 1760. H. 3 ft. 1½ in., W. 1 ft. 11½ in. *Croft Lyons Bequest.* W.56–1962

72 ARM-CHAIR. Carved walnut, upholstered in green leather. A design for a 'Garden Chair' with a somewhat similar back carved with bulrushes was published in Chippendale's *Director*, 3rd edition, 1762. The arms may be later additions. H. 3 ft. 1 in., W. 2 ft. W.46–1952

73 CHAIR. Carved mahogany, covered with green velvet. A particularly good example of the rococo Gothic taste. About 1760. H. 3 ft. 9½ in., W. 2 ft. W.13–1960

74 ARM-CHAIR. Carved mahogany upholstered with modern velvet. This and W.61a–1962 form part of a set of twenty-four chairs and two settees formerly at Ditton Park and were presumably made for George Brudenell, 4th Earl of Cardigan. A set of eight chairs of exactly the same design are at Blair Castle, and these were supplied by John Gordon of Swallow Street in

1756. They were described as '8 mahogany chairs, carv'd frames in fish scales, with a french foot and carv'd leaf upon the toe'. They cost just under £4 each. About 1756. H. 3 ft., W. 2 ft. 4 in. *Claude Rotch Bequest.* W.61–1962

75 ARM-CHAIR. Carved mahogany. Closely corresponds with a design dated 1759, in Chippendale's *Director*, 3rd edition, 1762, plate XXII, one of the designs for 'French Chairs' which does not occur in 1st edition, 1754. About 1760. (The damask is modern.) H. 3 ft. 6 in., W. 2 ft. 5 in. *Given by Brigadier W. E. Clark, C.M.G., D.S.O.*   W.47–1946

76 ARM-CHAIR. Carved mahogany, upholstered with modern yellow damask. In the 'French' fashion. About 1760. H. 3 ft. 2½ in., W. 2 ft. 4 in., D. 2 ft. 2½ in. *Given by Brigadier W. E. Clark, C.M.G., D.S.O., through the National Art-Collections Fund.*   W.8–1961

77 CHAIR. Carved mahogany. Back filled with lattice-work, legs and stretchers decorated with frets; in the 'Chinese' taste. (Cf. Chippendale's *Director*, 1754, plates XXIII–XXV.) About 1755–60. H. 3 ft. 4 in., W. 1 ft. 10½ in.

W.13–1911

78 CHILD'S ARM-CHAIR. Beech with parquetry of walnut and sycamore. Back and arms filled with lattice-work; inlaid with chequer and key patterns. About 1760–65. H. 2 ft. 7¾ in., W. 1 ft. 9⅜ in. *Given by Mr Randolph Behrens.*

884–1901

79 CHAIR. Carved mahogany. One of a pair. About 1765. Bears some resemblance to the designs of Robert Manwaring, author of the *Cabinet and Chair Makers' Real Friend and Companion*, 1765. H. 3 ft. 3 in., W. 2 ft. *Given by Mr Frank Green.*   W.9–1932

80 ARM-CHAIR. Turned and carved yew. 'Windsor' type, in the 'Gothick' taste. Mid 18th century. H. 3 ft. 3½ in., W. 1 ft. 11 in. *Bequeathed by Mrs S. I. Woodley.*   W.12–1940

81 ARM-CHAIR. Carved mahogany, the seat upholstered in contemporary needlework. About 1760. *One of a pair bequeathed by Lady W. S. Theobald.*

W.12–1938

82 ARM-CHAIR. Carved and gilded wood. Removable back. Upholstered in modern blue damask. An early attempt to produce a chair embodying neo-classical features. About 1765. H. 3 ft. 2 in., W. 2 ft. 4 in.   W.14–1967

83 ARM-CHAIR. Carved and gilded beechwood. Made by Thomas Chippendale. From a suite of furniture consisting of eight arm-chairs and four sofas designed in 1764 by Robert Adam for Sir Lawrence Dundas' London house at 19 Arlington Street. (The designs are in the Soane Museum, *Adam*, Vol. 17, No. 74.) Adam charged £5 'To a design of sofa chairs for the salon' on the 18th July, 1765. The suite was executed by Thomas Chippendale and his bill, for '8 large Arm Chairs exceeding richly carved in the Antick manner and Gilt in oil Gold Stuffed and cover'd with your own Damask and Strong Castors on the feet' came to £160.

The four sofas cost £216 and were all provided with leather cases lined with flannel and crimson checked linen covers. The bill was dated July 9th, 1765.

Three sofas and four chairs still remain at Aske Hall, Yorkshire, the seat of the Marquess of Zetland, descendant of Sir Lawrence Dundas.

This chair, which is one of Adam's most successful furniture designs, is stamped VII. H. 3 ft. 6 in., W. 2 ft. 6½ in. W.1–1937

84 PRESIDENT'S CHAIR. Carved and inlaid mahogany, upholstered in green leather. About 1770. H. 5 ft. 10 in., W. 2 ft. 3 in. W10.–1923

85 ARM-CHAIR. Mahogany. The splat pierced and carved with a vase and honeysuckle ornament. About 1770. H. 3 ft. 2¼ in., W. 1 ft. 503–1907

86 CHAIR. Carved mahogany, with lyre-shaped splat. One of a set, designed by Robert Adam, in the Eating Room at Osterley Park House. The original drawing is in the Soane Museum (*Adam*, Vol. 17, No. 93). About 1770. H. 3 ft., W. 1 ft. 8½ in. O.P.H.171–1949

87 ARM-CHAIR. Carved mahogany, with a splat composed of a lyre with patera and honeysuckle motives. One of a set, probably designed by John Linnell, in the Breakfast Room at Osterley Park House. About 1775. H. 2 ft. 11 in., W. 2 ft. 0¼ in. O.P.H.294–1949

88 ARM-CHAIR. Veneered with rosewood, inlaid with satinwood and other woods; cane seat; ormolu medallion and swags. Squab cushions covered with green leather. One of a set probably designed by John Linnell, in the Library at Osterley Park House. About 1770. H. 2 ft. 11 in., W. 2 ft. 0¾ in.
O.P.H.266–1949

89 ARM-CHAIR. Carved mahogany with metal strings, modern upholstery. John Linnell and Robert Adam had used the classical lyre as a splat in furniture designed by them, but this chair could well have been made under the influence of François Hervé, who worked for Henry Holland at Carlton House. About 1775. H. 2 ft. 10½ in., W. 1 ft. 11 in. 43–1869

90 ARM-CHAIR. Carved and gilded wood with upholstery of modern damask. About 1775. H. 3 ft. 5 in., W. 2 ft. 1 in. W.42 1946

91 ARM-CHAIR. Carved mahogany; back with 'Gothic' arcading. About 1775. H. 3 ft., W. 2 ft. 1 in. *Given by Mr Edward Dent.* W.21–1922

92 CHAIR. Carved mahogany, with 'Ladder-back'. About 1775. This type of back was first introduced in the late Stuart period and revived in the middle of the eighteenth century. The legs represent the last phase of the cabriole as shown in Hepplewhite's *Guide*, 1788. H. 3 ft. 1½ in., W. 2 ft. 0½ in. *Given by Mr Eric M. Browett in memory of his wife.* W.72–1937

93 ARM-CHAIR. Carved mahogany, with Prince of Wales's feathers. About 1775. The motive of the Prince of Wales's feather is found in Hepplewhite's *Guide*, 1st edition, 1788, plate 8 (cf. also, No. 105). H. 3 ft. 2½ in., W. 2 ft.
1458–1904

94 ARM-CHAIR. Carved and gilded. One of a set in the Tapestry Room at Osterley Park House. The tapestry covers woven by Neilson at the Gobelins factory in 1775, to match the wall-hangings. The chairs, possibly designed by Robert Adam, have close affinities with contemporary French models. H. 3 ft. 2 in., W. 2 ft. 1½ in. O.P.H.59–1949

95 ARM-CHAIR. Carved, gilded and upholstered with sprigged satin. The back supported by winged sphinxes. One of a set, designed by Robert Adam,

in the State Bedroom at Osterley Park House. For the original drawing see
No. 96. H. 3 ft. 3¾ in., W. 2 ft. 1 in.   O.P.H.42–1949

96 Design for an arm-chair for the State Bedroom at Osterley Park House, by
Robert Adam; dated 24th April, 1777. The drawing is in the Soane
Museum (*Adam*, Vol. 17, No. 97). See No. 95.

97 ARM-CHAIR. Carved mahogany. One of a set of nine acquired by
Jonathan Pytts for his house, Kyre Park, Worcestershire, 1776–81. About
1775–80. H. 3 ft. 3 in., W. 1 ft. 10½ in.   W.2–1946

98 ARM-CHAIR. Beechwood, painted to represent satinwood, and decorated
with green paint and an inlay of green stained wood; cane seat. The squab
cushion, which is not in place, covered with floral taffeta. One of a set at
Osterley Park House, probably designed and made by John Linnell. About
1779. H. 3 ft., W. 2 ft.   O.P.H.116–1949

99 ARM-CHAIR. Painted beechwood, with caned seat. One of a set, designed
by Robert Adam, in the Etruscan Room at Osterley Park House. The
original drawing, dated March 6th, 1776, is in the Soane Museum (*Adam*,
Vol. 17, No. 95). The squab is covered with pale grey silk. H. 2 ft. 11¾ in.,
W. 2 ft. 2¼ in.   O.P.H.10–1949

100 ARM-CHAIR. Mahogany painted black and ivory with decorative detail
in colour. About 1780–85. H. 3 ft. 1¼ in., W. 1 ft. 11 in.   W.52–1946

101 CHAIR. Carved mahogany. The turned and fluted legs headed with lotus
cappings. About 1785. H. 3 ft. 1 in., W. 1 ft. 10 in.   W.68–1935

102 CHAIR. Mahogany, carved with classical ornament and inset with a panel
of painted satinwood. About 1785. H. 3 ft. 1½ in., W. 1 ft. 8 in.   510–1907

103 CHAIR. Mahogany, inlaid with boxwood paterae. The splat closely
resembles a design in Hepplewhite's *Guide*, 1st edition, 1788, plate 4.
H. 3 ft., W. 1 ft. 8 in. *Given by Mrs A. R. Hatley.*   W.19–1934

104 ARM-CHAIR. Satinwood, painted in colours. This arm-chair is from a set
of painted satinwood supplied by Seddon, Sons and Shackleton to Elisha
Tupper, of Hautville House, Guernsey, in about 1790. H. 3 ft. 0½ in.,
W. 1 ft. 8⅞ in. *Given by Mrs A. E. Ingham.*   W.1–1968

105 CHAIR. Carved mahogany. The back is based almost exactly on George
Hepplewhite's *Guide*, 1st edition, 1788, plate 1 (right). H. 2 ft. 11 in.,
W. 1 ft. 9 in. *Given by Mr Eric Browett in memory of his wife.*   W.70–1937

106 ARM-CHAIR. Painted beechwood; the slats decorated with wheatear
motives. At Osterley Park House. About 1790–1800. The leather squab
cushion is not in place. H. 3 ft. 11 in., W. 2 ft.   O.P.H.216–1949

107 ARM-CHAIR. Carved mahogany, with inlaid stringing on the splat.
Covered with leather at a more recent date. About 1795–1800. H. 2 ft.
10 in., W. 1 ft. 1½ in.   W.6–1950

108 ARM-CHAIR. Turned beech, with decoration 'japanned' in black and
gold. About 1800. H. 2 ft. 9¼ in., W. 1 ft. 10⅛ in.   999–1897

109 ARM-CHAIR. Wood carved in relief and painted black, with gilded detail.
In the 'Egyptian' taste. Probably from a set made in 1806 for Frome Abbey.
Based on a design dated 1804, published in George Smith's *Household*

Furniture, 1808, plate 56 (cf. No. 110). H. 3 ft., W. 2 ft. 1¾ in. *Bequeathed by Mr Edward Knoblock.*   W.14–1945

110 Design for an arm-chair from George Smith's *Household Furniture*, 1808, plate 56 (cf. No. 109).

111 ARM-CHAIR. Grained and gilded, with upholstered seat and back. One of a pair. Based on a design by Thomas Hope in *Household Furniture*, 1807, plate 22. H. 3 ft. 6 in., W. 2 ft. 3 in.   W.49–1949

112 ARM-CHAIR. Beechwood, carved and gilded, and 'japanned' dark green. Female terminal figures in the 'Grecian' taste. Compare with designs for 'drawing room chairs' in George Smith's *Household Furniture*, 1808, pl. 55 (above). About 1810. H. 2 ft. 10½ in., W. 2 ft.   W.5–1939

113 CHAIR. Beech, japanned black and gilded with brass enrichments. Caned seat. About 1810. H. 2 ft. 10 in., W. 1 ft. 6 in.   W.2–1958

114 ARM-CHAIR. Carved mahogany, original leopard skin upholstery. Ensuite with a single chair W.4–1967. Stamped with the initials IM/D. Two other chairs from the same suite, now in the Metropolitan Museum, New York, are dated 1811 and 1820. H. 3 ft. 7½ in., W. 2 ft. 3 in.

W.3–1967

115 FLY CHAIR. Beech, carved, painted and gilded, designed by Philip Hardwick and made by W. & C. Wilkinson for the Court Drawing-Room at the Goldsmith's Hall. About 1834.   W.1–1964

116 ARM-CHAIR. Carved and gilded mahogany, from a set made for the drawing room at Eaton Hall, Cheshire, probably to the design of William Porden. About 1823. H. 3 ft. 1 in., W. 2 ft. 1 in. *Acquired with the funds bequeathed by Mrs Blanche Redbern Clayton.*   W.22–1959

117 CARVER CHAIR. Carved oak upholstered in imitation leather, designed by A. W. N. Pugin (1812–52) for Charles Scarisbrick of Scarisbrick Hall, Lancashire. About 1837. One of a set of six dining and two carver chairs. H. 3 ft. 7½ in., W. 1 ft. 6½ in.   Circ. 236–1951

118 CHAIR. Carved and turned mahogany in the 'Elizabethan' style, with an embroidered back and seat in tent-stitch. About 1845. H. 3 ft. 3 in., W. 1 ft. 5 in.   Circ. 241–1960

119 ARM-CHAIR. Carved and gilded wood with the original velvet upholstery, in the Gothic style. About 1830. H. 3 ft. 10½ in., W. 2 ft. 5 in. *Given by Mrs Gilbert Russel.*   W.42–1950

120 ARM-CHAIR. Walnut, carved and ornamented with marquetry and set with a Worcester porcelain plaque of Prince Albert. Made by Henry Eyles of Bath and shown at the Great Exhibition of 1851. H. 3 ft. 8½ in., W. 3 ft. 8 in. *Given by William Stanley Eyles, Esq.*   Circ. 35–1958

121 ADJUSTABLE BACK CHAIR. Ebonized wood with turned decoration upholstered in the 'Bird' woollen tapestry. Adapted by Philip Webb from an old Sussex chair and made by Morris & Co. from about 1866. H. 3 ft. 2½ in., W. 2 ft. 4 in.   Circ. 250–1961

122 ARM-CHAIR. Stained wood with rush seat. Designed by D. G. Rossetti, and made by Morris & Co. about 1865. H. 2 ft. 11 in., W. 1 ft. 7½ in.

Circ. 304–1961

123 CHAIR. Oiled wainscot oak upholstered in natural leather, the back stamped in gold. Designed by E. W. Godwin (1833–86) and made by the Art Furniture Co., London, for Dromore Castle, Ireland, about 1867. H. 3 ft. 6¾ in., W. 1 ft. 9 in.

Circ. 719–1966

124 ARM-CHAIR. Mahogany inlaid with rosewood and sycamore. Part of a suite designed for James Mason of Eynsham Hall, Oxford, about 1872, by Owen Jones (1809–74). H. 2 ft. 8¼ in., W. 2 ft. *Given by the Home Office.*

Circ. 34–1954

125 CHAIR. Ebonized birch, carved and inlaid, with leather seat and back. Probably designed by B. J. Talbert (1838–81) about 1865. Made by Doverston, Bird & Hull, Manchester. H. 2 ft. 11 in., W. 1 ft. 5½ in.

Circ. 314–1963

126 ARM-CHAIR. Mahogany with cane back, sides and seat, and loose cushions covered in the Tulip chintz designed by William Morris in 1875. The chair made by Morris & Co. about 1893, and probably designed by George Jack (1855–1932). H. 3 ft. 1 in., W. 2 ft. 0½ in. *Bequeathed by Miss Amy Tozer.*

Circ. 249–1961

127 ARM-CHAIR. Ash ladder-back with rush seat. Designed by Ernest Gimson (1864–1919) about 1888. H. 4 ft. 1½ in., W. 1 ft. 10 in.   Circ. 232–1960

128 CHAIR. Oak with upholstered seat. Designed by C. R. Mackintosh 1868–1928) and exhibited at the Vienna Secession Exhibition, 1900. About 1900. H. 4 ft. 6 in., W. 1 ft. 7½ in. *Given by the Glasgow School of Art.*

Circ. 130–1958

129 ARM-CHAIR. Oak inlaid with ebony, with panels of rush in the seat and back. Designed by E. G. Pannett and made by William Birch & Co. Ltd., High Wycombe, in 1901. H. 2 ft. 9¾ in., W. 2 ft. 4 in.   Circ. 400–1959

ILLUSTRATIONS

1. From a French illumination. About 1400

2. Second quarter of the 16th century

3. Second quarter of the 16th century

4. Dated 1574

5. Late 16th century

6. Early 17th century?

Elizabethan-carved oak armchair of Glastonbury
type ≈1600

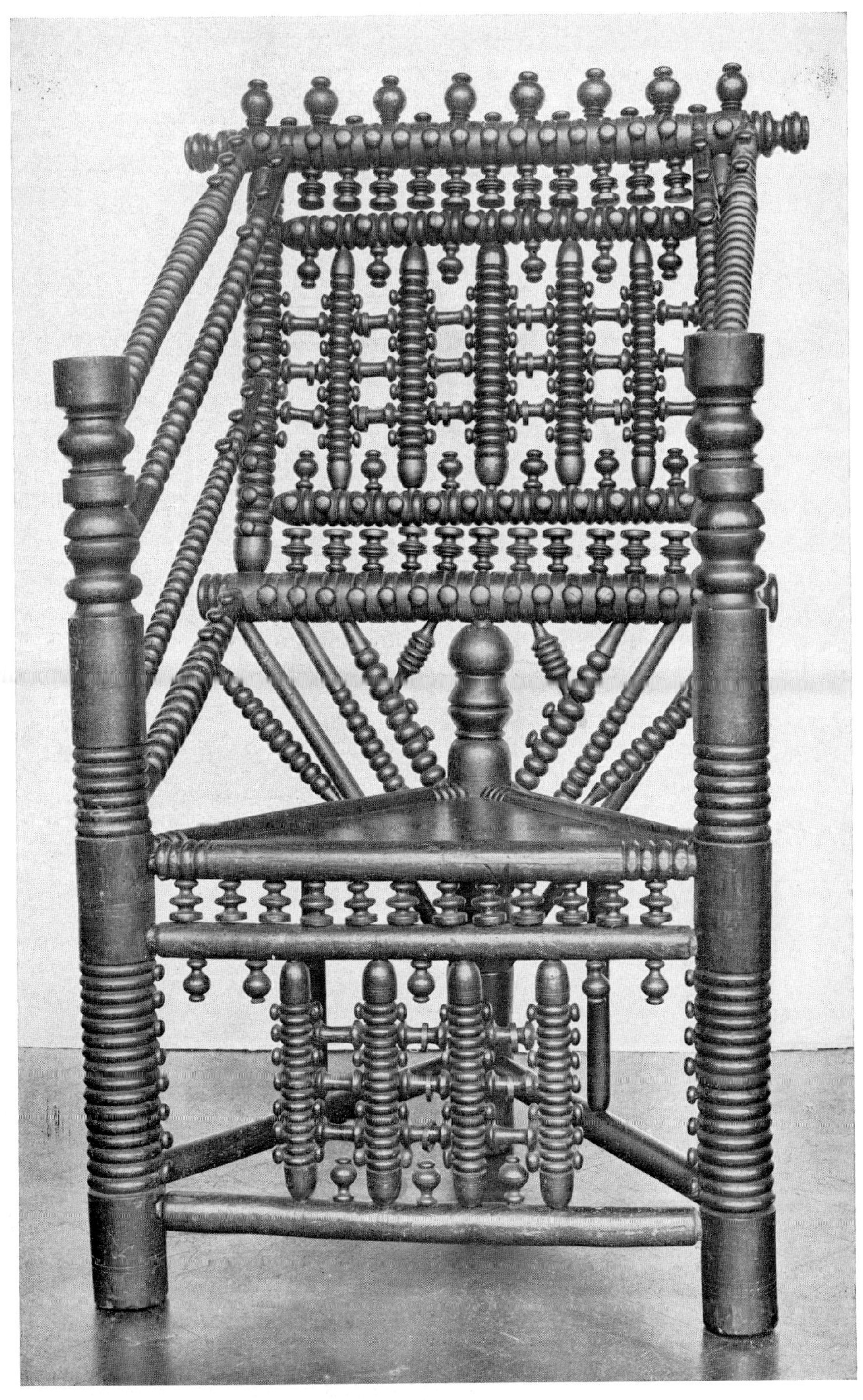

7. Early 17th century?

Elizabethan - turned ash roak chair

8. About 1600

9. First quarter of the 17th century

Elizabethan

10. First quarter of the 17th century

11. First quarter of the 17th century

Early Jacobean

12. Second quarter of the 17th century

13. Second quarter of the 17th century

Early Jacobean- frame entirely covered in fabric

14. Second quarter of the 17th century

15. Second quarter of the 17th century

16. About 1640

17. Dated 1641

18. Mid 17th century

19. About 1660

20. The cover worked between 1641 and 1655. The frame about 1660

21. About 1660

22. About 1670

23. About 1675

24. About 1675

LATE JACOBEAN - PAINTED + PARCEL GILT ARMCHAIR
CARVED WITH DOLPHIN MOTIFS

25. About 1675

LATE JACOBEAN – CARVED + GILT WOOD SLEEPING
CHAIR WITH ADJUSTABLE BACK

26. About 1680

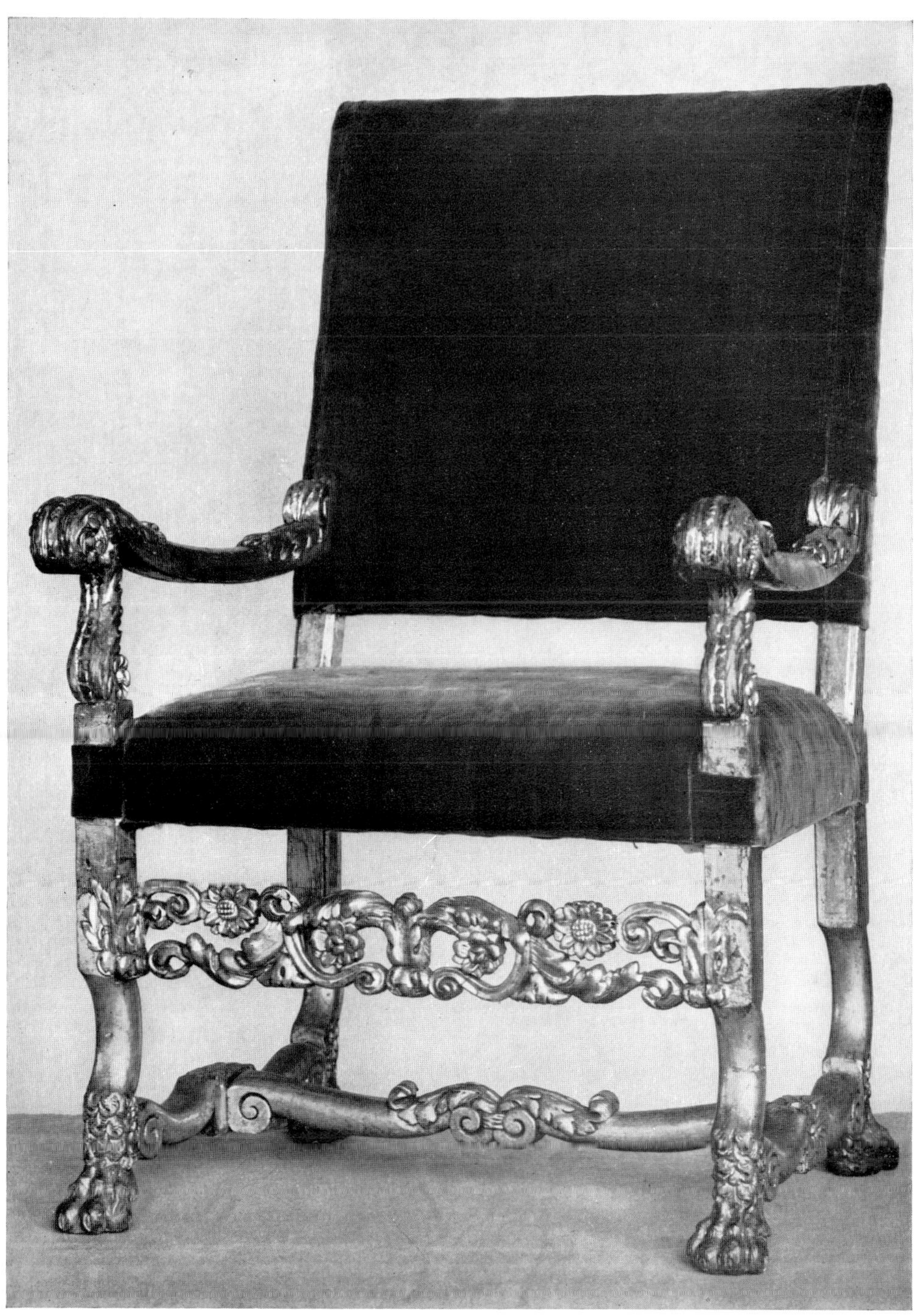

27. About 1680

28. About 1680

29. About 1680

LATE JACOBEAN - CARVED & TURNED WALNUT
ARMCHAIR OF RESTORATION TYPE

30. About 1685

31. About 1685

32. About 1685

33. About 1690

34. About 1690

William + Mary - carved walnut chair

35. About 1695

36. About 1700

37. About 1700

38. About 1700

39. About 1710

40. About 1710

41. About 1715

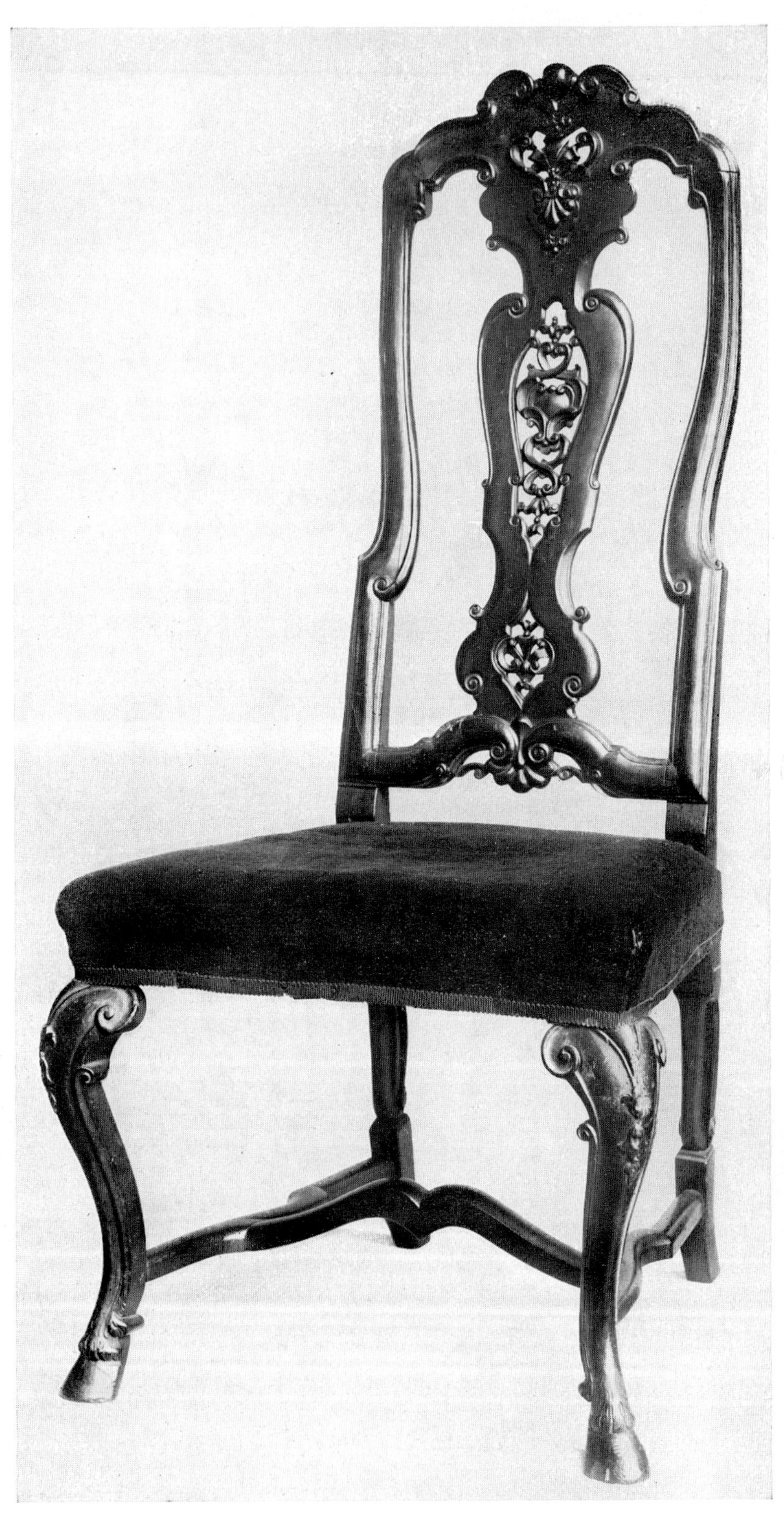

42. About 1717

William + Mary - carved walnut chair

43. About 1717

44. Second decade of the 18th century

45. About 1720

46. About 1720

47. About 1720

Queen Anne

48. About 1725

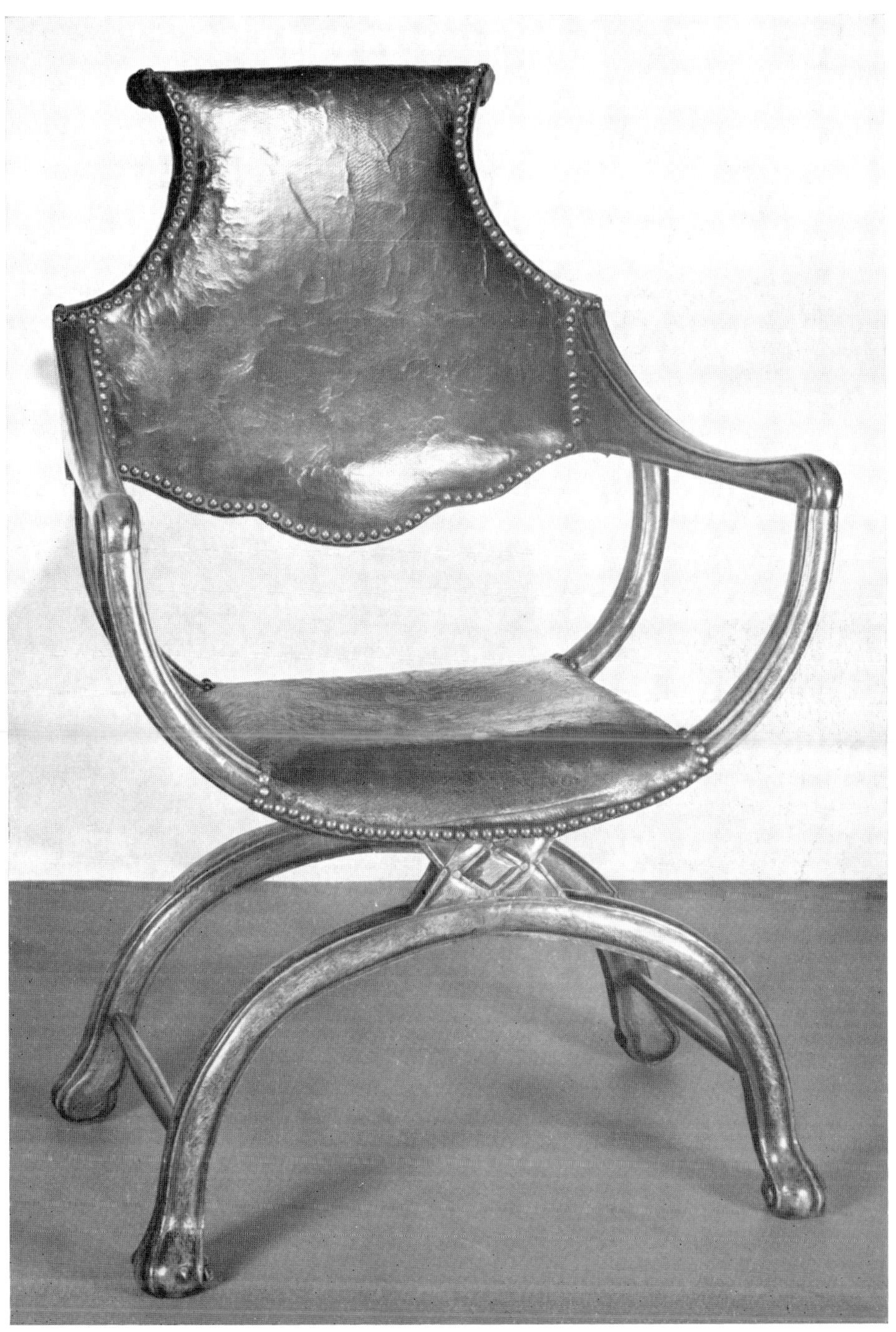

49. About 1720

50. About 1725

Georgian - Carved walnut Corner

51. About 1725

52. About 1725

53. About 1725

Georgian

54. About 1730–35

55. About 1740

56. About 1730

57. About 1725–30

58. About 1730

59. About 1725–30

60. About 1740

61. About 1745

62. Mid 18th century

63. Mid 18th century

64. Mid 18th century

65. About 1750

66. Mid 18th century

67. Mid 18th century

68. About 1755

69. Design from Chippendale's *Director*, 1754 edition

70. About 1755

71. About 1760

72. About 1760

73. About 1760

74. About 1756

75. About 1760

76. About 1760

77. About 1760

78. About 1760–65

79. About 1765

80. Mid 18th century

81. About 1760

82. About 1765

83. About 1764

84. About 1770

85. About 1770

Hepplewhite - carved mahogany
camel back

86. About 1770

87. About 1775

88. About 1770

89. About 1775

90. About 1775

91. About 1775

92. About 1775

Hepplewhite - ladder back

93. About 1775

Hepplewhite - Prince of Wales Feathers

94. About 1776

95. About 1777

96. Design by Robert Adam, dated 1777

97. About 1775–80

98. About 1779

99. About 1776

100. About 1780–85

101. About 1785

102. About 1785

103. About 1790

Hepplewhite · carved mahogany ror boxwood paterae

104. About 1790

Hepplewhite - Satinwood armchair w/ painted decoration

105. About 1795

Sheraton-carved mahogany chair

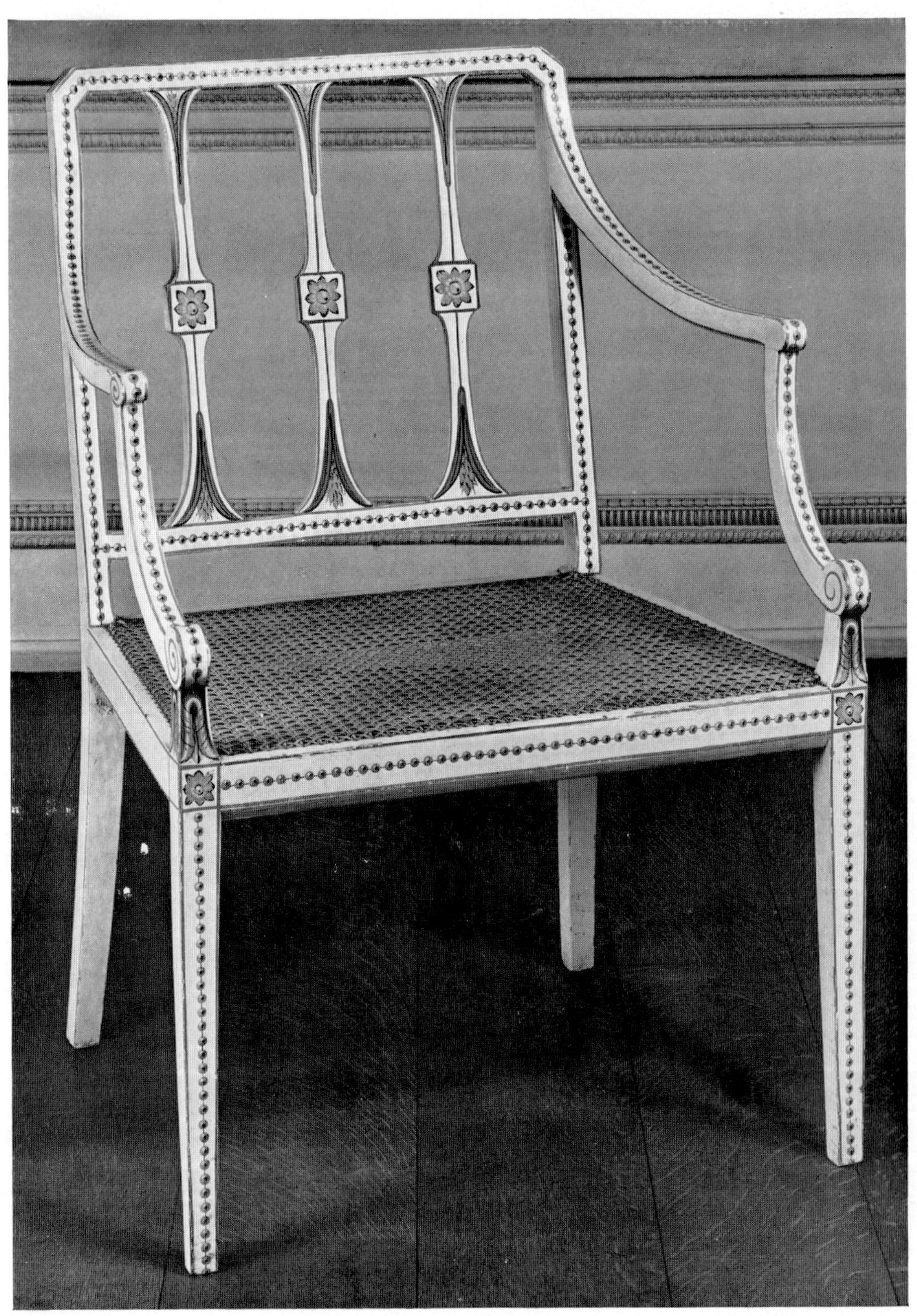

106. About 1790–1800

107. About 1795–1800

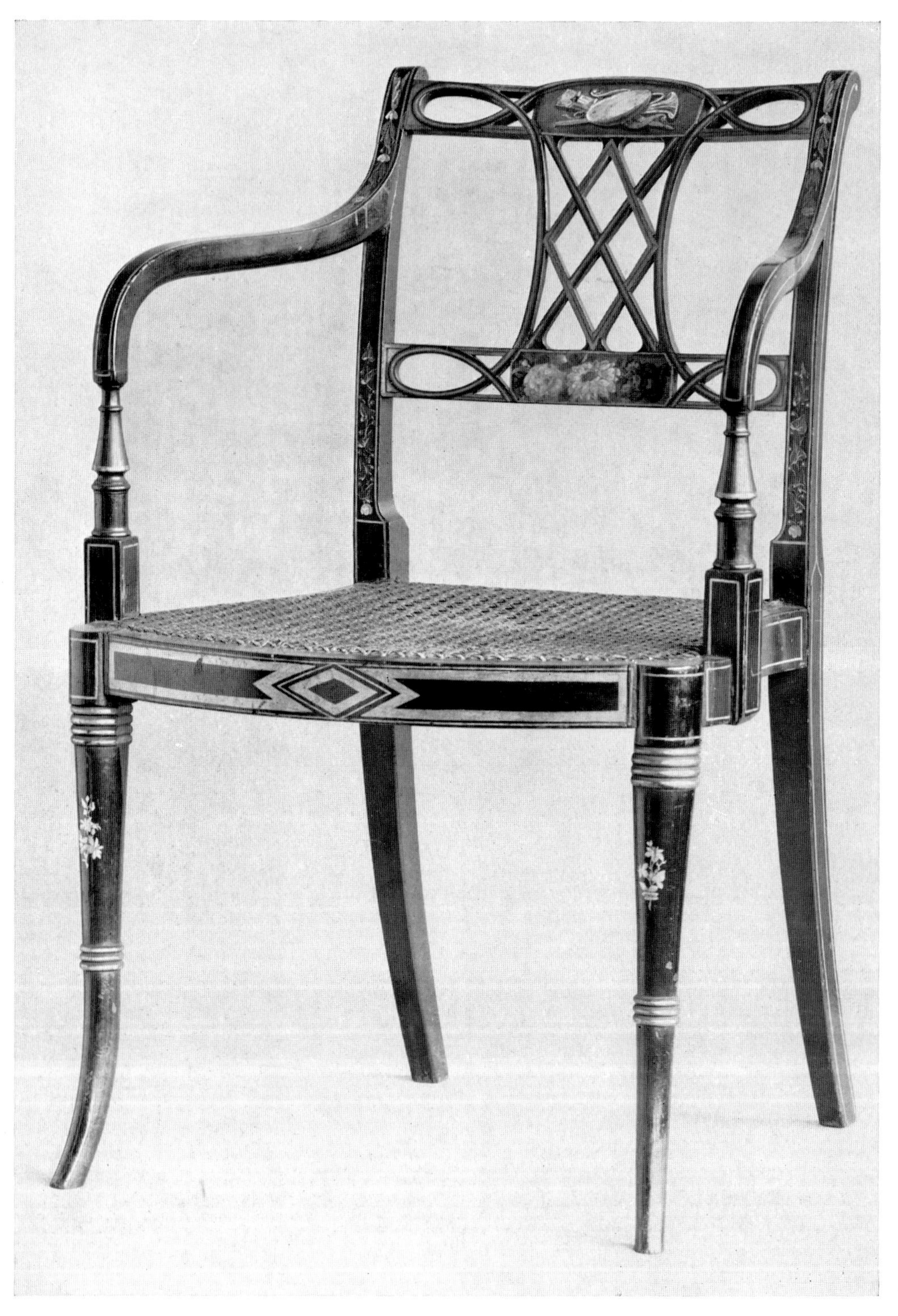

108. About 1800

Sheraton - turned beechwood. japanned in black and gold

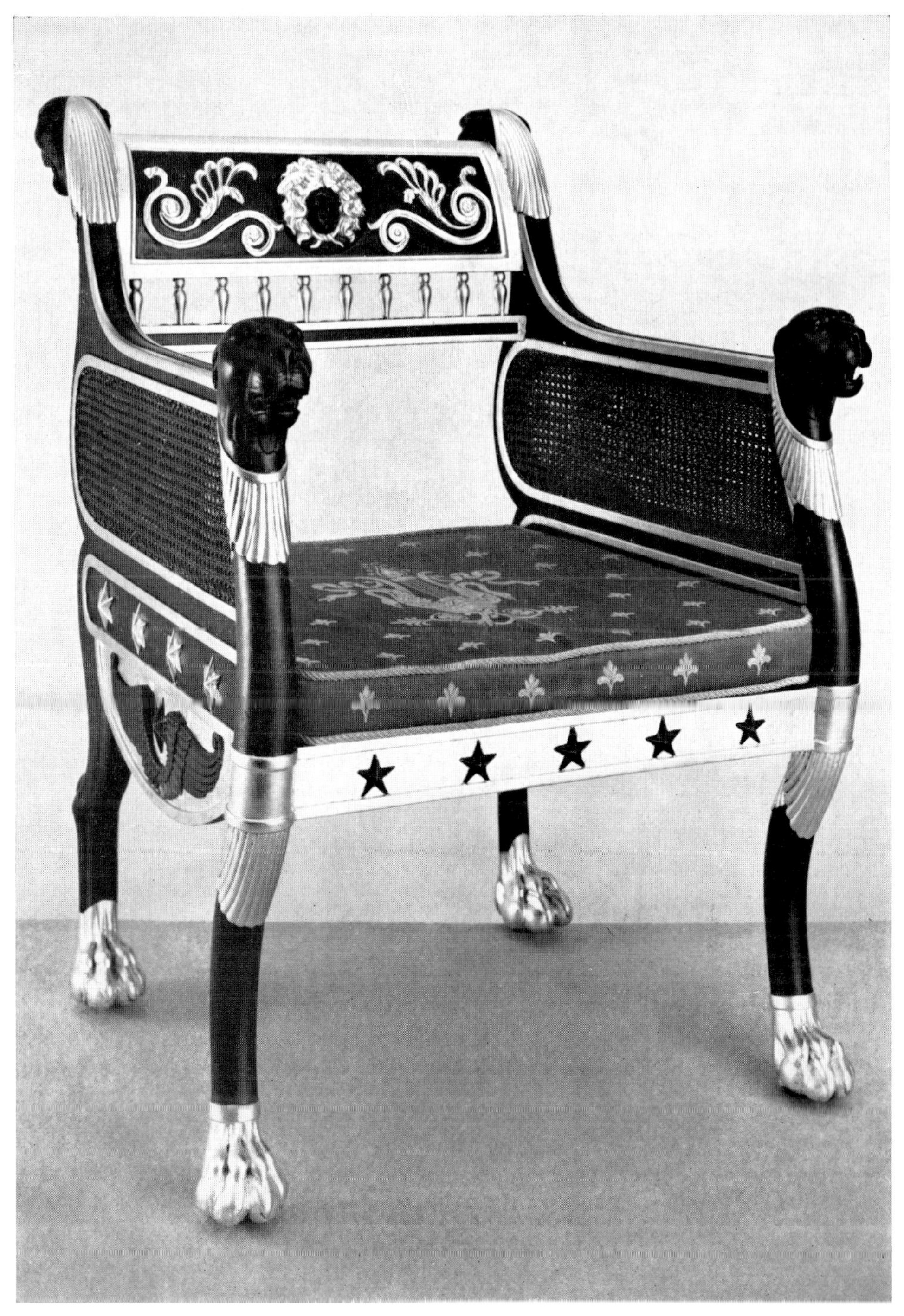

109. Made in 1806

Regency - painted black and gilt - detail in Egyptian taste

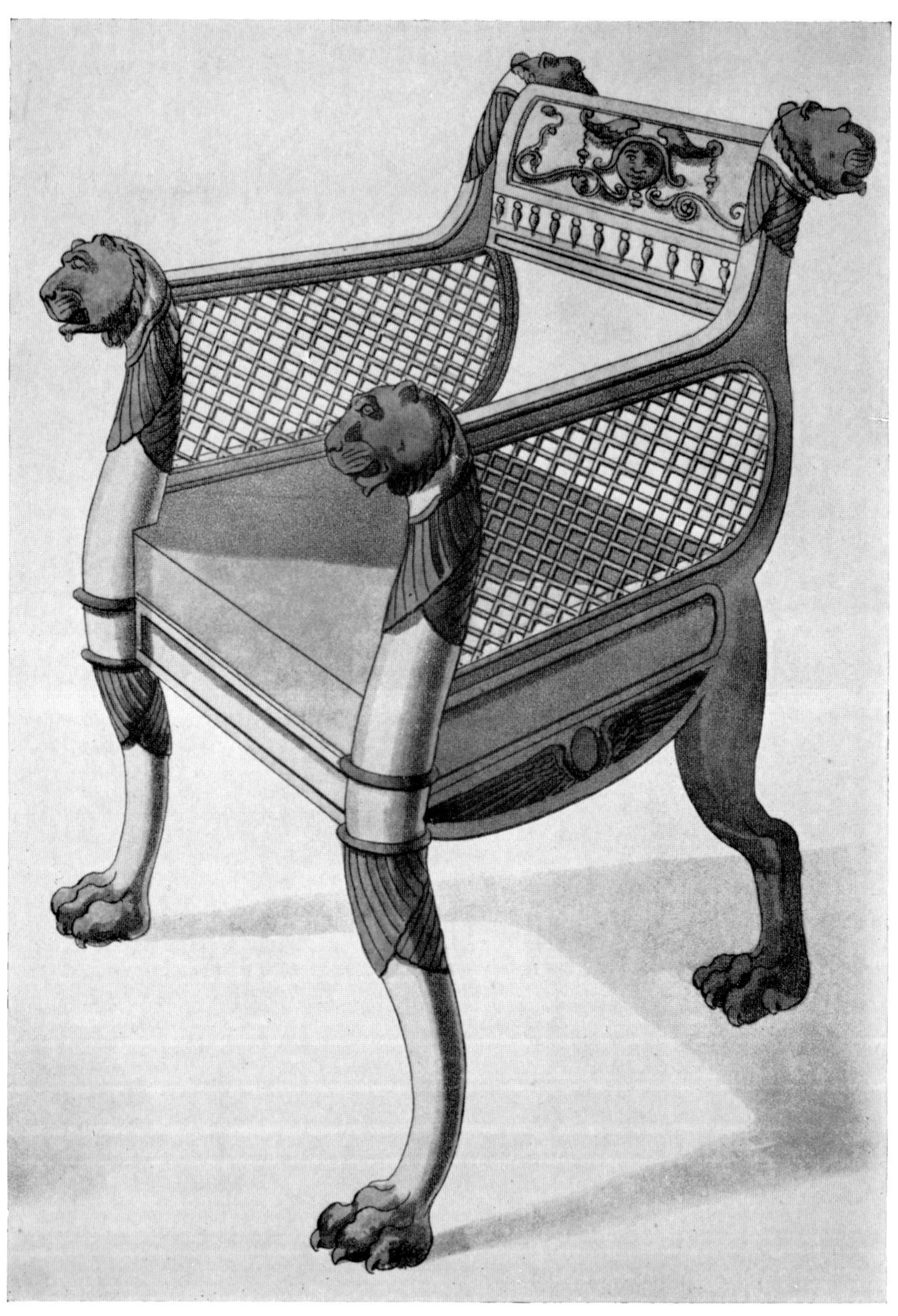

110. Design from George Smith's *Household Furniture*, 1808. Dated 1804

111. About 1807

112. About 1810

Regency - carved beechwood, japanned in dark green w/ gilt detail. Female terminal figures in Grecian taste.

113. About 1810

114. About 1820

115. About 1834

116. About 1823

117. About 1837

118. About 1845

119 About 1830

120. About 1850

121. About 1866

122. About 1865

123. About 1867

124. About 1872

125. About 1865

126. About 1893

127. About 1888

128. About 1900

129. About 1901